THE NEGRO NATIONAL COLONIAL QUESTION

By

NELSON PEERY
General Secretary,
Communist Labor Party
of the United States of North America

First Ed. 1972 prepared by the Communist League of America
2nd Revised Edition, April 1978

Originally published by
Workers Press, Chicago
Reprinted with permission of the author by
Red Star Publishers, 2015
www.RedStarPublishers.org

TABLE OF CONTENTS

Introduction		1
Definitions		3
Chapter 1:	Latifundist (Capitalist) and Patriarchal (Pre-capitalist) Slavery and the Evolution of the Negro Nation	13
Chapter 2:	The Civil War in the United States of North America; Its Aims, Causes and Results	22
Chapter 3:	From the Negro Bourgeois Democratic National Movement to the Negro People's National Liberation Movement	28
Chapter 4:	National Evolution and the Negro Nation	58
Chapter 5:	Marxism and the National Colonial Question	85
Chapter 6:	Theoretical Deviations on the Negro National Colonial Question	89
Chapter 7:	Imperialist Oppression of the Negro Nation and the South as a Region	103
Chapter 8:	The Negro National Minority in the Anglo-American Nation	117
Chapter 9:	The Anglo-American Minority in the Negro Nation	126
Chapter 10:	Conclusion	131

Appendix

Introduction	133
Resolutions of the Communist International on the Negro Question in the United States	134
From *The People's Tribune:* Negro History Week—Socialism: The Only Road	160
From *The People's Tribune*: Education Column—Are There 'Races?'	167
From *The People's Tribune:* Education Column—What Are National Minorities?	169
Statistics on the Economic and Social Status of Negroes in the USNA	172
Footnotes	182
Index	187

ACKNOWLEDGEMENTS

Much of the work on this book was a collective effort of research and editing. Without the hard work and support of the following people this book would probably never have gone into print at this time. The political editing of this edition was undertaken by Comrades Marlene, of the Communist Labor Party's National-Colonial Commission, and Deby and Larry of the People's Tribune. Copy editing was undertaken by Comrades Phyllis and Bill. And my appreciation goes to Elinor of the Workers Press staff for coordinating all the aspects of publication.

N. Peery
November, 1975

ABOUT THE AUTHOR

Nelson Peery grew up in rural Minnesota, the son of a postal worker in the only African-American family in town. Hoboing across the Western United States supplemented his education during the Great Depression. It was an experience about racism and the American economy that no school could teach.

Since the original publication of "The Negro National Colonial Question" in October 1975, Peery has written numerous other articles, pamphlets, and books, including: "African-American Liberation and Revolution in the United States" (1992); "Entering an Epoch of Social Revolution" (1993); "Black Fire: The Making of an American Revolutionary" (1994); "The Future Is Up to Us: A Revolutionary Talking Politics With the American People" (2002); and "Black Radical: The Education of an American Revolutionary" (2007). In January 2000, the pamphlet "Moving Onward: From Racial Division to Class Unity" by Brooke Heagerty and Nelson Peery was published.

Born in 1923, Nelson Peery has spent over 70 years in the revolutionary movement, writing and speaking about African-American liberation, the global economy, and a vision of a new, cooperative America. In 1993, he was one of the founding members of the League of Revolutionaries for a New America. He can be reached by e-mailing cobas8@earthlink.net.

INTRODUCTION

The Communist Labor Party of the USNA, from its inception, has recognized the critical importance of the Negro question. A review of the history of revolutionary movements will show that a revolutionary disregards the Negro question at his peril. We know that the historic facts of the development of the Anglo-American working class militated against a clear comprehension of the Negro question. Today, we have no such excuses.

Until the late 1920's the Anglo-American proletariat was formed primarily from the importation of German, Irish, Italian and Slavic workers. It is only natural that the struggle of these workers should be couched in the framework of the struggles within their native lands. There is no Negro question in Germany or Poland, so it is only natural that these immigrants—many of them revolutionaries—would disregard the burning Negro question. And it is only natural that the capitalist class would recognize this abnormal situation and take advantage of it. We Anglo-American revolutionaries have a terrible debt to pay to history. We must begin by clarifying history and taking it out of the hands of the capitalist class and making it into a weapon of the proletariat. This is the basic reason for this document.

Life is hardly the "bowl of cherries" that we have been taught. On the contrary, life is dialectical and therefore difficult to live and understand. We have attempted to make this document an accurate reflection of life—therefore it cannot be read as most of the inaccurate, immature and shallow movement documents. This statement is meant to be studied.

There are certain seemingly insurmountable difficulties that will be encountered. One of these is the contradiction between words, which are static and concepts, which are constantly in motion. We try to resolve this contradiction by giving you a rather extensive list of definitions. The limitations of the English language force us to give some words a specific meaning by definition.

As in all circumstances, the Communist Labor Party of the USNA welcomes the comradely criticism of the readers.

This collective effort represents the fundamental position of the Central Committee of the Communist Labor Party of the USNA. It is a reaffirmation of the position of the Communist International and the position of V. I. Lenin and J. V. Stalin, the greatest of all thinkers on the question of oppressed peoples and nations.

This document should also be seen as a polemic against the positions of all "left" social chauvinists and principally against the revisionism of the Communist Party of the U.S.A.

DEFINITIONS

The State of the United States of North America

The state of the United States of North America is the basic organ of violence and repression in the hands of the Anglo-American imperialist bourgeoisie. This state arose from and was based on the consolidation of the original separate 13 states. The USNA is a multi-national state, comprised of the imperialist oppressor nation, the Anglo-American nation (which consists roughly of the northern east, midwest and western regions); its direct colonies, the Negro Nation and Puerto Rico; the oppressed Southwest region; and the Philippines, in fact a direct colony with a separate sham "state" tied openly and directly to the USNA imperialists. In addition this State exercises its dictatorship over a number of peoples, including the Mexican national minority, the Indian peoples, the Alaskan Eskimos, the Aleutian and Hawaiian peoples. It has reduced to "dependencies" Samoa, Canton and Enderbury Islands, Guam, Pacific Islands under provisional U.S. administration (sixty islands), Palmyra Island, Howland, Baker, Jarvis and Wake Islands, the Corn Islands, the Swan Islands, the Virgin Islands. It has taken the Panama Canal Zone from the Panamanian people. It is properly referred to as the USNA to differentiate it from the United States of Mexico or United States of Brazil, etc.

Anglo-America

The primary basis of culture in the Anglo-American Nation is English. In the development of the history of the nation, successive waves of non-English, European peoples populated the USNA. On a primary level these non-English peoples were compelled to adopt the Anglo culture. In this process, the melting pot concept emerged. The various European peoples injected certain aspects of their national culture in the process of assimilating the Anglo. Specific aspects of the Anglo-American culture evolved, chemically as well as mechanically mixing the aspects of the European, African and the Indian cultures.

The other aspect of the development of Anglo-America was the concrete specific conditions that faced these English and Europeans upon their arrival in North America. They came from relatively developed nations, especially the English, but they were met in North America with a relatively low level of the productive forces and vast open land. In their struggle of conquest against the Indian peoples and in the harshness and isolation of frontier life, a specific national culture was developed on the Anglo-European base; thus it became not merely Anglo-European, but Anglo-American.

The territorial frontiers of the Anglo-American Nation are generally the Canadian frontier to the north to the Atlantic sea coast on the east; proceeding from the Canadian frontier south to the beginnings of the area associated with the plantation belt in Delaware. The border then proceeds west along the northern edge of the area associated with the plantation system. This line proceeds generally west and south in an inverted arc into Texas and south into the Gulf of Mexico. The western frontier proceeds south from the Canadian border along the Pacific Coast to the area generally associated with the struggles of the Mexican national minority. The border then proceeds in a north-easterly direction to the north of Denver, connecting to the Gulf of Mexico to the east of San Antonio, Texas. Within this national territory, there are numerous autonomous areas that belong to the Indian people whose economic, territorial and political rights have yet to be restored.

The exact delineation of the frontier must be set by economic and population factors that cannot be known today.

Basically, the Americas can be divided into the general categories of Anglo and Hispanic America. These general areas represent a base of Anglo or Hispanic cultures for the emergence of national cultures that were conditioned by the evolution of history in each specific country.

Although the total of the Western Hemisphere is referred to as the Americas, the United States of North America is the only country that defines itself as America in reference to nationality. Other nations refer to themselves first by national definition such as Argentinean, Brazilian, Canadian, Dominican, etc., and only in the most general sense as American.

To a great degree such concepts arose because of the overwhelming presence and determining power of USNA imperialism. The peoples of the Americas correctly see the chauvinism in referring to the USNA as "America."

The situation is further complicated by the obvious fact that the Canadians are just as much Anglo-American as the peoples of the USNA. The only difference in definition being that the Canadians designate themselves as Canadians, whereas the peoples of the

USNA use the national designation of American. Thus the term is used in two senses—hemispheric and national.

American Exceptionalism

American exceptionalism is the shallow revisionist "theory" that United States of North American capitalism is an exception to Marxist economic and social laws.

This "theory" was introduced into the communist movement by Jay Lovestone as General Secretary of the CPUSA, by Earl Browder as General Secretary of the CPUSA and by William Z. Foster as Chairman of the CPUSA. The material base for this "theory" was the fact that the economic cyclical crisis was not as severe, widespread or lengthy in the USNA as in Europe. The obvious reason for this was the fact that each crisis was marked by a further expansion of the Western frontier and by the homesteading of public lands. The unemployed proletariat and the ruined businessmen "went West" to start over, thereby relieving the population pressure, creating a market and mitigating the effects of crisis. The theory of American exceptionalism was disproved by the great depression of 1929 when there was very little public land left and the full and severe effects of the crisis were felt from 1929 to the beginning of the Second World War.

Imperialism

Lenin defined imperialism as: "1) the concentration of production and capital has developed to such a high stage that it has created monopolies which play a decisive role in economic life; 2) the merging of bank capital with industrial capital, and the creation, on the basis of this 'financial capital,' of a financial oligarchy; 3) the export of capital as distinguished from the export of commodities acquires exceptional importance; 4) the formation of international monopolist combines which share the world among themselves; and 5) the territorial division of the whole world among the biggest capitalist powers is completed. Imperialism is capitalism in that stage of development, in which the dominance of monopolies and finance capital has established itself, in which the export of capital has acquired pronounced importance, in which the division of the world among the international trusts has begun, in which the division of all territories of the globe among the biggest capitalist powers has been completed."(1) By the end of World War II the USNA imperialists had emerged as the most powerful and aggressive of all imperialists. The financial capitalists of the USNA, relying on the fears of the European and Asian imperialists that the international communist revolution was at hand, gathered all imperialism under their protection.

On the other hand, and much more importantly, the USNA imperialists emerged from the war with a financial stranglehold on all the imperialists and were able to force a regrouping of all these imperialists under the domination of USNA imperialism. The last act of serious inter-imperialist struggle was the Anglo-French invasion of the Suez in 1956. Since then, the camp of world imperialism has been regrouped, fully dominated and headed by USNA imperialism. In a word, a large powerful section of financial capital is no longer characterized by national interests. Imperialism today is characterized by internationalization, not only in the sense of international exploitation, but also by international ownership.

Primitive Accumulation

"The accumulation of capital pre-supposes surplus-value; surplus value pre-supposes capitalist production; capitalist production presupposes the pre-existence of considerable masses of capital and of labor power in the hands of producers of commodities. The whole movement, therefore, seems to turn in a vicious circle, out of which we can only get by supposing a primitive accumulation preceding capitalist accumulation; an accumulation not the result of the capitalist mode of production, but its starting point." Further, "the so- called primitive accumulation, therefore, is nothing else than the historical process of divorcing the producer from the means of production. It appears as primitive, because it forms the pre-historic stage of capital and of the mode of production corresponding with it." And finally, "in the history of primitive accumulation, all revolutions are epoch-making that act as levers for the capitalist class in course of formation; but, above all, those moments when great masses of men are suddenly and forcibly torn from their means of subsistence, and hurled as free and 'unattached' proletarians on the labor-market. The expropriation of the agricultural producer, of the peasant, from the soil, is the basis of the whole process."(2)

Along with the robbery of the peasant, was the brutal slave trade and the wholesale murder of the Indians which all contributed to primitive accumulation.

6

Revisionism

Revisionism is a doctrine hostile to Marxism within Marxism. Lenin says that what happened to Marx happened to all revolutionary thinkers, that is, "After their death, attempts are made to convert them into harmless icons, to canonize them, so to say, and to surround their names with a certain halo for the 'consolation' of the oppressed classes and with the object of duping the latter, while at the same time emasculating the essence of the revolutionary teaching, blunting its revolutionary edge and vulgarizing it. At the present lime, the bourgeoisie and the opportunists within the working class movement concur in this 'doctoring' of Marxism. They omit, obliterate and distort the revolutionary side of his teaching, its revolutionary soul. They push to the foreground and extol what is or seems acceptable to the bourgeoisie." Further, "revisionism, or 're-vision' of Marxism, is today, one of the chief, if not the chief, manifestations of bourgeois influence on the proletariat and bourgeois corruption of the workers."(3) Today in the USNA the revisionists are best exemplified by the CPUSA who, as agents of the bourgeoisie, inject their revisionism into the working class and channel the revolutionary aspirations of the workers into reformist programs leading them always to defeat and into the hands of the bourgeoisie. Revisionism does not arise from the working class, but rather is injected into the class by the bourgeois intellectuals, trade union officials and their copartners, the CPUSA.

Neo-colonialism

Neo-colonialism is the indirect control of a country through control of its economic structure and a puppet political apparatus. Semi-colonial countries are countries in political upheaval in which the democratic forces have seized political power. At this point, neither the relations of production nor the owners of the means of production have been altered. The attitude of the semi-colonial government toward these questions will determine if the country progresses toward freedom from all capital and toward socialism, or lapses back into a neo-colonial status—a status of domination by imperialism in another form.

White Supremacy

White supremacy was a theoretical justification for acts of primitive accumulation and colonization of the colored peoples.

White supremacy grew with Anglo-American expansionism. So long as there was no real economic use for white supremacy in the U.S.N.A., or rather in the English colonies, it did not develop. It was only with the need to clear the western parts of the original colonies that the concept of white supremacy arose. With the development of chattel slavery in the South, a new rationale other than bringing the Africans here to make Christians of them was needed; then the concept of white supremacy slowly emerged. In practice, white supremacy is mainly based on color discrimination, i.e., "the whiter you are, the better you are."

Semi-colony

In attempting to define semi-colony we must quote Lenin from *Imperialism, the Highest Stage of Capitalism:* "The semi-colonial state provides an example of the transitional forms which are to be found in all spheres of nature and society... The semi-colonial countries provide a typical example of the 'middle stage.' It is natural that the struggle for these semi-dependent countries should have become particularly bitter in the epoch of finance capital, when the rest of the world has already been divided... Since we are speaking of colonial policy in the epoch of capitalist imperialism it must be observed that finance capital and its corresponding foreign policy, which reduces itself to the struggle of the Great Powers for the economic and political division of the world give rise to a number of transitional forms of state dependence. Typical of this epoch is not only the two main groups of countries; those owning colonies and colonies, but also the diverse forms of dependent countries which, officially, are politically independent, but in fact are enmeshed in the net of financial and diplomatic dependence—the semi-colony."(4) We can see that today, for instance, the states of Southern Yemen, Tanzania, Zambia and the Allende period of Chile are examples of semi-colonies. The economies of these countries are dependent on foreign finance capital. The administrative aspect of the state (i.e., legislature, parliament, etc.) is temporarily in the hands of the petty bourgeois democratic forces. In most cases the military and other state institutions are still in the hands of the reactionaries and imperialists. However, the status of semi-colony is a temporary, transitional stage. The petty bourgeois democratic forces want to pause and erect a bourgeois national state under their hegemony. However, under the epoch of imperialism, this is not possible. Either the revolutionary state must continue on to so-

8

cialism, led by the proletariat, or become a neo-colony controlled by the imperialists.

Anglo-European
This term refers to those peoples who are of English or European descent. Some of these peoples immigrated and others were forced to immigrate. Some came to the South as slaves or indentured servants and most of those who came to the Anglo-American Nation were unskilled laborers.

National Chauvinism
It is the ideology that states that one nation is superior to others and thus helps to maintain the domination of one nation over another. Chauvinism is a concept that does away with class outlooks and substitutes the national imperialist outlook.

White Chauvinism
Because of the specific role of white supremacy in the history of the USNA, amongst the various forms of national chauvinism, the most brutal and aggressive form is white chauvinism. It provides the excuse for the brutal exploitation of the colored nations and peoples of the world; it is a form that the social bribery takes to the Anglo-American people that prevents the unity of the working class; it is the principal ideology of aggressive USNA fascism.

W. Z. Foster
One-time leader of the CPUSA. As an author and theoretician he was a leading international syndicalist and revisionist. One of his best known theoretical concepts is that of "American Exceptionalism" in the realm of the national question. He developed a cultural- nationalist line in regard to the Negro Nation with his theory of a "nation within a nation." By doing this, he absolved the CPUSA from defining territorial boundaries and thus played into the hands of the imperialists by allowing the continuation of the enslavement of the nation; for without boundaries, "where is the nation?"

Dred Scott Case
Dred Scott was a Negro held a slave in Missouri. In 1834 he was taken to Fort Snelling, Minnesota, in free territory and he re-

mained there, on free soil, for four years. In 1838, Scott was returned to Missouri and held again as a slave. He sued for his freedom and it went to the U.S. Supreme Court. Chief Justice Roger B. Taney declared that Scott was not a citizen, but a slave. He ruled that Negroes were inferior to Anglo-Americans, that they could be justly reduced to slavery for their own benefit, that they "had no rights which a white man was bound to respect," and that they were not, and could not become part of the Anglo-American people, even when accorded the right to vote.

Thirteenth Amendment—December 18, 1865
1. Neither slavery nor involuntary servitude, except as a punishment for crime whereof the party shall have been duly convicted, shall exist within the United States, or any place subject to its jurisdiction.

2. Congress shall have power to enforce this article by appropriate legislation.

Fourteenth Amendment—July 28, 1868
All persons born or naturalized in the United States, and subject to the jurisdiction thereof, are citizens of the United States and of the State wherein they reside. No State shall make or enforce any law which shall abridge the privileges or immunities of citizens of the United States; nor shall any State deprive any person of life, liberty, or property without due process of law, nor deny to any person within its jurisdiction the equal protection of the laws.

Fifteenth Amendment—March 30, 1870
1. The right of the citizens of the United States to vote shall not be denied or abridged by the United States or by any State on account of race, color or previous condition of servitude.

2. The Congress shall have power to enforce the provisions of this article by appropriate legislation.

Negro
The word Negro is used in different contexts and means different concepts depending on history and place. Shortly after the discovery of the Americas, the Portuguese and Spanish, probing down the coast of Africa, became involved in the already developed slave trade in Africa. At that time the word Negro meant only "black", the

literal translation from the Spanish. Centuries later, as slavery became a major industry in the United States of North America, the word Negro began to have a different meaning. The slaves in the USNA had been drawn from a variety of peoples in Africa. Injected into and among the African slaves were a number of Indian peoples and, of course, tens of thousands of slaves of partial African and partial Anglo-European descent. The slavers' lash soon did away with any distinction between the descendant of the Congo and the light-skinned illegitimate son of the driver man. Based on the specific conditions of slavery in the USNA, there arose the Negro people—a historically evolved people, socially and culturally developed from the framework of slavery.

By the end of the 19th century, the word Negro again began to change its meaning. Owing to the specifics of the rise of USNA imperialism and the history of the Black Belt of the South, there arose a nation, oppressed by USNA imperialism, whose social root and base was the aforementioned Negro people. The term Negro developed to include a national meaning. The confusion around the term arises because nations are not extensions of tribes and are not based on color, etc., but on history. Now, when referring to the nation, we use the term Negro and mean national and not color. In the same manner, when one speaks of the French we do not differentiate between the members of the French nation who are Basque, Lombardi or Goth, or the basic root of the nation—the Frankish peoples. We can only ask the reader to be a dialectician and differentiate when we write Negro as a historically evolved people who were slaves, or, on the other hand, when we say Negro meaning national, referring to all the people residing in the historically evolved community of territory that we call the Negro Nation. In the sense of national, Negroes are both the "black" majority and "white" minority.

Negro Nation

The Negro Nation is that historically evolved stable community of Negro people, along with the historically developed Anglo-American minority, who live in the Black Belt and the economically dependent area of the Southern USNA. This nation, which evolved from the specifics of slavery, is a historically evolved stable community of people formed on the basis of a common language, territory, economic life and psychological make-up manifested in a

11

common culture.

The nation is referred to as the Negro Nation because the base of that nation is the Negro people who evolved as a people prior to the evolution of the Negro Nation.

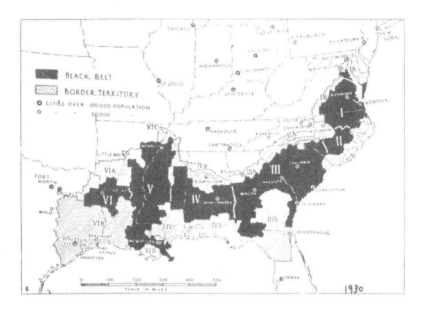

Black Belt and Border Territories

Source: James S. Allen, The Negro Question in the United States, (New York: International Publishers, 1936)

CHAPTER ONE

LATIFUNDIST (CAPITALIST) AND PATRIARCHAL (PRE-CAPITALIST) SLAVERY AND THE EVOLUTION OF THE NEGRO NATION

Everything, including the growth of the Negro Nation, is rooted in the past. Therefore, it is necessary to get a clear perspective and understanding of the past in order to understand the present.

The Negro question as a specific of social motion and class struggle in the United States of North America, is rooted in the type of slave system which developed in the Black Belt. Therefore, it is essential that we understand why slavery in the Black Belt was what it was, in order to understand why the Negro Nation and the Negro liberation struggle exist in their present forms.

A comprehensive study of slavery in the Western Hemisphere would fill volumes. Such a study would be beyond our intent. Rather, this section will be limited to an examination of what slavery in the Black Belt was.

The revisionists and the "left-wing" pro-capitalist enemies of the Negro people have been forced to cling to the conception that slavery in the USNA was feudalism, or patriarchal slavery, and no significant section of the Marxist movement has taken the position of Marx in the examination of the economic relations of that institution. Marx wrote:

> In the second type of colonies—plantations—where commercial speculations figure from the start and production is intended for the world market, the capitalist mode of production exists, although only in a formal sense, since the slavery of Negroes precludes free wage labour, which is the basis of capitalist production. But the business in which slaves are used is conducted by *capitalists.*(1)

Further, Marx says, "where the capitalist outlook prevails, as on American plantations, this entire surplus-value is regarded as profit..."(2)

Feudalism and patriarchal slavery are not value producing systems. The patriarchal slave system is devoted to the production of the immediate means of subsistence.

A part of the problem of the revolutionaries seeing that "in the modem world, it [slavery] results in the capitalist mode of production,"(3) is that it is taken out of its historical and geographic environment. Why slavery in the new world? Because it was impossible to get labor. Why should a free man toil in the hot sun for 12 to 18 hours a day for another? Who would labor in the fetid snake-infested swamps of Alabama if it were possible to secure one's own free land just to the west? Slavery was necessary because of the free land and shortage of labor. However, chattel slavery did not prevent the slave from engaging in capitalist production with all the social and historical consequences.

What were the conditions of slavery in the Black Belt area of the Southern USNA? In general, slavery in the USNA was justified by the rationale of white supremacy. Strict segregation, not only between white and black, but between field hands and house servants was maintained. Black Belt slave-masters had a scientific knowledge (based on statistics published by organized slave owners' societies and insurance companies) of just how long a slave would last under given conditions. Masters used slave labor in a manner calculated to maximize profits. This practice made Black Belt slavery an indescribable horror.

This description of slavery based on capitalism in the Black Belt would not be complete without some indication of the life of overwork of the slave on the cotton plantation in the USNA. One of the best accounts comes from the celebrated work of Soloman Northrup:

> During all these hoeings the overseer or driver follows the slaves with a whip, such as has been described. The fastest hoer takes the lead row. He is usually about a rod in advance of his companions. If one of them passes him, he is whipped. If one falls behind or is a moment idle, he is whipped. In fact, the lash is flying from morning until night the whole day long...
>
> ...The hands are required to be in the cotton fields as soon as it is light in the morning, and, with the exception of ten or fifteen minutes, which is given them at noon to swallow their allowance of cold bacon, they are not permitted to be a moment idle until it is too dark to see and when the moon is full they often times labor till the middle of the night.(4)

Karl Marx also described the conditions of slavery in the USNA Black Belt:

The slave-owner buys his laborer as he buys his horse. If he loses his slave, he loses capital that can only be restored by new outlay in the slave-mart. But the rice-grounds of Georgia or the swamps of the Mississippi may be fatally injurious to the human constitution; but the waste of human life which the cultivation of these districts necessitates, is not so great that it cannot be repaired from the teaming preserves of Virginia and Kentucky. Considerations of economy, moreover, which, under a natural system, afford some security for humane treatment by identifying the master's interest with the slave's preservation, when once trading in slaves is practiced, become reasons for racking to the uttermost the toil of the slave; for, when his place can at once be supplied from foreign preserves, the duration of his life becomes a matter of less moment than its productiveness while it lasts. It is accordingly a maxim of slave management, in slave-importing countries, that the most effective economy is that which takes out of the human chattel in the shortest space of time the utmost amount of exertion it is capable of putting forth. It is in tropical culture, where annual profits often equal the whole capital of plantations, that Negro life is most recklessly sacrificed. (5)

In this period, Woodson and Wesley report that in the cotton belt a slave owner would have to purchase five slaves per year for every thirty he owned in order to maintain the original number. So severe were the working conditions that the slave women for the most part could not bear children.

The expression "sold down the river" had a dreadful meaning among the slaves in the areas bordering the Black Belt to the North. These areas, especially Virginia and Kentucky, were slave breeding areas. Farm production was primarily for the local market so conditions in the field were tolerable. Whenever a slave trader from the Black Belt appeared on these farms, there was terror in the slave quarters, for all the slaves knew they could expect a short, hard life "down the river." In fact, the average life expectancy of a slave in the border areas was 55 years. In the Black Belt, the average was only seven years of labor.

Source: Langston Hughes & Milton Meltzer, A Pictorial History of the Negro in America, (New York: Crown Publishers, Inc., 1956.)

Slaves who began to work in the Black Belt fields at the prime age of 17 could be expected to live only seven years after that. Fifteen percent of the slave children died from overwork and maltreatment before they were nine years old.

Marx further explains slavery under capitalism:

> But as soon as people, whose production still moves within the lower forms of slave labour, corvee-labour, etc., are drawn into the whirlpool of an international market dominated by the capitalist mode of production, the sale of their products for export becoming their principal interest, the civilized horrors of overwork are grafted on the barbaric horrors of slavery, serfdom, etc. Hence the negro labour in the Southern states of the American Union preserved something of a patriarchal character, so long as production was chiefly directed to immediate local consumption. But in proportion, as the export of cotton became of vital interest to these states, the over working of the negro and sometimes the using up of his life in seven years labour became a factor in a calculated and calculating system.(6)

Source: Langston Hughes & Milton Meltzer, A Pictorial History of the Negro in America (New York: Crown Publishers, Inc., 1956)

Here, at one blow, Marx clearly sets forth the character of capitalist slavery in North America in distinction to the slavery in some other areas in the Americas. Marx says:

> It is, however, clear that in any given economic formation of society, where not the exchange value but the use value of the product predominated, the surplus-labour will be limited by a given set of wants which may be greater or less, and that here no boundless thirst for surplus-labour arises from the nature of the production itself. Hence in antiquity, over-work becomes horrible only when the object is to obtain exchange-value in its specific independent money-form; in the production of gold and silver. Compulsory working to death is here the recognized form of over-work. (7)

This was the situation in the mines of Peru, Bolivia, etc. While English ships transported the commodities of cotton, sugar, etc.—which reflected the commodity-capitalist production and wealth—Spanish ships transported little but gold, silver and precious stones. This is a reflection of Iberian feudalism whose commercial interest was limited to the money form of commodities.

In *The Poverty of Philosophy*, Marx shows the decisive role of slavery in the USNA in the development of capitalism:

> Direct slavery is just as much the pivot of bourgeois industry as machinery, credits, etc. Without slavery you have no cotton; without cotton you have no modern industry. It is slavery that has given the colonies their values; it is the colonies that have created world trade, and it is world trade that is the pre-condition of large-scale industry. Thus slavery is an economic category of the greatest importance.
>
> Without slavery, North America, the most progressive of countries would be transformed into a patriarchal country. Wipe out North America from the map of the world, and you will have anarchy—the complete decay of modern commerce and civilization. Abolish slavery and you will have wiped America off the map of nations.(8)

Further, in *Capital,* Marx continues,

> Whilst the cotton industry introduced child slavery in England, it gave in the United States a stimulus to the transformation of the earlier, more or less patriarchal slavery, into a system of commercial exploitation. In fact, the veiled slavery of the wage workers in Europe needed, for its pedestal, slavery pure and simple in the new world.(9)

It is clear that this "commercial exploitation" of the slave system in the USNA developed parallel with the rise of industrial capitalism. At the same time, slavery in the USNA was the wellspring of value so necessary for the development of capitalism. This marked slavery in the Black Belt as latifundist-capitalist slavery—in contrast to patriarchal pre-capitalist slavery of antiquity.

Capitalism is the commodity producing society where human labor itself appears on the market as a commodity. Simply because this labor must be sold all at once does not change the character of the exploitation of that labor. Marx points out:

Women and children at work in a cotton field.
Source: Langston Hughes & Milton Meltzer, A Pictorial History of the
Negro in America (New York: Crown Publishers, Inc., 1956)

The process of production, considered on the one hand
as the unity of the labour-process and the process of creating value, is the production of commodities; considered on
the other hand as the unity of the labour-process and the
process of producing surplus-value, it is the capitalist process of production, or capitalist production of commodities.(10)

From this point of view, the only possible conclusion is that
latifundist slavery in the USNA was capitalism, a commodity producing society, where the labor did not appear on the market as free
labor. Social systems do not appear in a vacuum and therefore none
have appeared in a pure form. It is the petty bourgeois intellectuals'
search for laboratory purity in social systems that has prevented
them (and through them prevented the revolutionaries) from seeing
the slavery in the Black Belt as slavery based on capitalism and,
therefore, exposing the secret of the genesis of the Negro National
Question.

A man pulls a plow as a woman guides it.
Source: Langston Hughes & Milton Meltzer, A Pictorial History of the
Negro in America (New York: Crown Publishers, Inc., 1956)

In fact, the hiring out of slaves was common practice in the
South.

Almost every railroad in the ante-bellum South was
built at least in part by bondsmen. In Georgia, they constructed more than a thousand miles of roadbed. In 1858, a
Louisiana newspaper concluded: Negro labor is fast taking
the place of white labor in the construction of southern railroads.

Until the 1840's, the famed Tredegar Iron Company in
Richmond used free labor almost exclusively. But in 1842,
Joseph R. Anderson, then commercial agent of the company, proposed to employ slaves as a means of cutting labor
costs. The board of directors approved of his plan, and
within two years Anderson was satisfied with "the practi-
cability of the scheme." In 1847, the increasing use of
slaves caused the remaining free laborers to go out on
strike, until they were threatened with prosecution for
forming an illegal combination. After this protest failed,

Anderson vowed that he would show his workers that they could not dictate his labor policies: he refused to re-employ any of the strikers. Thereafter, as Anderson noted, Tredegar used 'almost exclusively slave labor except as the Boss men. This enabled me, of course, to compete with other manufacturers.'(11)

The objective conditions of the production of cotton and tobacco, the constant clearing of the land, the harsh conditions of life of the workers, the frontiers and free land, all demanded un-free labor to feed the whirlpool of international commercial intercourse. The form was slavery; the content was capitalism.

When chattel slavery was brought to an end by the Civil War there was no possibility of the slave population merging into the mainstream of Anglo-American life. The conditions of a labor shortage; an international demand for cotton; a starving, defenseless ex-slave population allowed for—no, *forced*—the continuation of segregation, rule by terror and a return to the field driven almost as brutally as before, but this time as sharecroppers and hired hands instead of slaves. These international and local conditions laid the foundation for the emergence of the modern Negro Nation.

CHAPTER TWO

THE CIVIL WAR IN THE UNITED STATES OF NORTH AMERICA

Its Aims, Causes and Results

Due to the confusion that still persists regarding the causes and effects of the Civil War in the USNA, the editors are putting forth Marxist conclusions regarding the war. Serious students of the war should study the articles and letters of Marx and Engels on the war. The richest source is *The Civil War in the United States,* by Karl Marx and Frederick Engels.

Above and beyond all other considerations, the Civil War was, as Marx wrote, "a war of conquest for the extension and perpetuation of slavery."(1) It is in this sense of the word that Marx and Engels pointed out that the Civil War was a war between two social systems. They point out how the Union was of service to the slave oligarchy only so long as it served the slave system. As the contradictions between capitalist production with slave labor and capitalist production with free labor intensified, and the balance of political power tilted against the slave system, it became clear that 20,000,000 free men would no longer submit to the dictatorship of the 300,000 slave masters who controlled the country.

> ...In 1860, there were in the South 385,000 owners of slaves distributed among 1,516,000 free families. Nearly three-fourths of all free Southerners had no connection with slavery through either family ties or direct ownership. The 'typical' Southerner was not only a small farmer, but also a non-slaveholder.
>
> ...Slightly less than half of the slaves belong to approximately twenty-five thousand masters operating plantations of [large] dimensions.(2)

It was at this point that the slave oligarchy first attacked the South and subdued it and then attacked the North.

The Aims of the Contending Forces

The slave oligarchy understood that if secession was attained by the core of deep Southern slave states, the economic and social interests of the entire Mississippi basin and even of California would compel them to join the slavery Union. Marx points out their aim was to reorganize the Union on the basis of slavery, not to dissolve it. The inevitable result of such a reorganization would be the introduction of slavery for the Anglo-American workers of the North and West. On the side of the Union, all the moral and political forces that were generated by the long hard struggle of the yeoman farmers momentarily joined forces with the financial and industrial bourgeoisie against the restrictive dictatorship of the slaveocracy.

The farmers who could not compete against slave labor readily joined the struggle. The workers, who as a result of competition from slave production were being forced down to the level of slavery themselves, also joined the fight. The industrial and financial bourgeoisie, drunk with their new political and financial power, rushed into the battle. In history, the underlying economic causes are always covered up by surface, ideological proclamations. *The Battle Hymn of the Republic,* with its fevered "As He died to make men holy, let him die to make men free," became the clarion call of the Union forces.

John Brown, in his long struggle to force the South to secede from the Union, knew that the gigantic economic forces of the North would be the trump card to force the South back into the Union without slavery. What started as a reactionary war of conquest was, for a historical moment, turned into a true revolution—the slaveocracy fighting to hold back the wheels of progress, the forces of the Union objectively fighting to free the means of production from the fetters that slave landlordism had placed upon them.

As Karl Marx wrote:

> Direct slavery is just as much the pivot of bourgeois industry as machinery, credits, etc. Without slavery you have no cotton; without cotton you have no modern industry. It is slavery that has given the colonies their value; it is the colonies that have created world trade, and it is world trade that is the pre-condition of large-scale industry. Thus slavery is an economic category of the greatest importance.(3)

So we see that at a point in its growth, slavery, which made the colonies of value, became the fetter on the further development of the productive forces. Thus, it was overthrown. It was not the morality of the anti-slave movement that was fundamental, but it was the conflict between these two forms of capitalist production that made the "irrepressible conflict" explode into what at that time was the bloodiest and costliest conflict in history.

The Political Motion that Precipitated the War

Historically, it is clear that the election of Lincoln was the signal for the secession of the Confederate states. However, that begs the question: what allowed for the election of Lincoln?

Lincoln was elected because of the political growth of the Northwest. The growth of the Northwest caused a split in the Democratic Party and the result was the election of Lincoln. How did this take place?

First of all, the economics of slavery, which were based on cotton which rapidly depleted the soil, demanded the constant expansion of slavery into fresh and fertile soils. This meant the westward motion of the slave system. Since the Executive and Judicial branches of the government were firmly in the hands of the slavers, the only struggle that could take place was in the Legislative Branch. The slave oligarchy slowly eroded the power of the House of Representatives and made the Senate the more powerful body because the North became, by far, the more populous. But that also meant that as new territories became states they had to go into the slavers' political pocket. This was easily accomplished in Texas and New Mexico. In Missouri (1820), the famous compromise was worked out wherein Missouri entered the Union as a slave state, but slavery was excluded west of the Missouri River and north of 36 degrees 30 minutes latitude. Then, in 1854, hard-pressed to expand slavery, the Southern dominated legislature and the Senate passed the Kansas-Nebraska Bill which repealed the Missouri Compromise and left it up to the citizens of the territories to decide whether or not they wanted the slave system When it became apparent that the free soil immigrants and yeoman farmers were capable of fighting for their rights against slavery, the oligarchy had to try again. John Brown and his men were the best example of the capabilities of the free men to resist slavery. A huge relief organization was formed to arm and protect the freemen from the murder and intimidation of the border ruffians, who were the vanguard of the slavers. Kansas was saved for free labor. Out of this struggle and this relief organization grew the Republican Party.

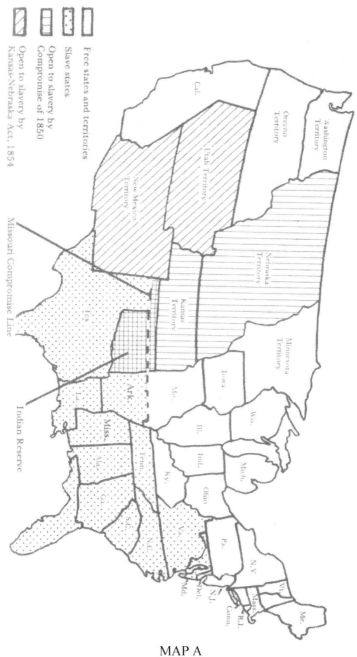

Free states and territories

Slave states

Open to slavery by Compromise of 1850

Open to slavery by Kansas-Nebraska Act, 1854

Missouri Compromise Line

Indian Reserve

Cal.

Oregon Territory

Washington Territory

Utah Territory

New Mexico Territory

Nebraska Territory

Kansas Territory

Minnesota Territory

Tex.

Iowa

Mo.

Ark.

La.

Wis.

Ill.

Ind.

Mich.

Miss.

Ala.

Tenn.

Ky.

Ohio

Ga.

S.C.

N.C.

Va.

Pa.

N.Y.

Md.

Del.

N.J.

Conn.

R.I.

Mass.

Vt.

Me.

MAP A
Free and Slave States

25

The slavers then turned to the base of their political strength—the Supreme Court. In 1857, the Supreme Court presented the Dred Scott decision. This infamous decision stated that the government had the duty to protect slave property in any territory. So, against the expressed will of the majority, all territories became slave territories. As Marx wrote:

> If the Missouri Compromise of 1820 had extended the geographical boundary-line of slavery in the Territories, if the Kansas-Nebraska Bill of 1854 had wiped out every geographical boundary-line and set up a political barrier instead, the will of the majority of the settlers, then the Supreme Court of the United States, by its decision of 1857, tore down even this political barrier and transformed all the Territories of the republic, present and future, from places for the cultivation of free states into places for the cultivation of slavery.(4)

The Supreme Court and the Executive Office under Buchanan sought to win in Washington what they had lost in battle with John Brown. Steven Douglas, leader of the Northern Democrats, broke with the South because the Dred Scott decision contradicted the principle of sovereignty as defined in the Kansas-Nebraska Bill of 1854. The Democratic Party was fundamentally split.

The Republicans at the second convention (1860) declared their platform was: not a foot of new territory is to be conceded to the slave empire. The irrepressible conflict was breaking out. At the Montgomery secessionist Congress (1860) a short time later, Senator Toombs, the leading spokesman for the South, said, "In fifteen years more, without a great increase in slave territory, either the slaves must be permitted to flee from the whites, or the whites must flee from the slaves."(5)

Thus the issue was joined. During the election of 1860, the Democrats got 2,223,110 votes, the Republicans got 1,866,452. But the Democratic vote was split. Douglas received 1,375,157 and Breckinridge, 847,953. Lincoln was elected, the Union was out of the hands of the oligarchy; and the slave power, wheeled from political activity, prepared a military Bonapartist coup and attacked the Union. Bleeding Kansas took her revenge. It was Kansas that birthed the Republican Party and split the Democrats, thus insuring the election of Lincoln and the resultant Civil War.

26

So we see that the Civil War was not an exceptional event in history, but a moment in history that completely conforms to the Marxist laws of social development.

AI the end of this costly and bloody affair, and during its epilogue, the period of Reconstruction, there emerged in the North a financial oligarchy whose blood lust and financial power put to shame the wildest dreams of the slavers. Dr. DuBois noted with sadness that "the South controlled the Nation and Wall Street controlled the South." The end result of the Civil War and the gigantic accumulation of financial capital and industrial means of production was the emergence of United States of North America imperialism, the scourge of finance capital. Its first creation and first victim of its savage gold lust was the defenseless and prostrate Negro Nation.

CHAPTER THREE

FROM THE NEGRO BOURGEOIS DEMOCRATIC NATIONAL MOVEMENT TO THE NEGRO PEOPLE'S NATIONAL LIBERATION MOVEMENT

Any real analysis of the Negro people's movement has to begin by seeing it as an integral part of the international revolutionary upsurge of the colonial peoples against imperialism. In the Communist Labor Party we use as our base the historic as well as the political conclusions of the October Revolution.

Stalin pointed out:

> Thus the October Revolution, having put an end to the old bourgeois movement for national emancipation, inaugurated the era of a new, socialist movement of the workers and peasants of the oppressed nationalities, directed against all oppression, which also means national oppression, against the rule of the bourgeoisie, their 'own' and foreign, and against imperialism in general.(1)

Further Stalin states:

> It became obvious that the emancipation of the toiling masses of the oppressed nationalities and the abolition of national oppression were inconceivable without a break with imperialism, without the overthrow by each of its 'own' national bourgeoisie and the assumption of power by the toiling masses themselves.(2)

It is obvious that no national bourgeoisie can successfully lead a movement of national liberation, just as it is obvious that in this period of its extreme parasitism, imperialism will not peacefully allow any colonial nation, especially a small nation, an independent existence.

Therefore, in our discussion of the Negro national movement we will divide history into two parts; 1) the period prior to the October Revolution in the Soviet Union which we call the Negro Bourgeois Democratic National Movement, and 2) the post 1917 period which we call the Negro People's National Liberation Movement. (In general, this division conforms to the whole of the colonial emancipation movement. However, the Negro People's

National Liberation Movement as such actually began more in 1922 than in 1917. Nevertheless, the shift in political forces was the result of the October Revolution.)

Due to years of confusion on the Negro question, it is necessary to answer the question, how and why did the Negro Bourgeois Democratic National Movement arise? We have already indicated the difference that existed between patriarchal slavery and slavery as it existed in the areas owned or controlled by the advanced capitalist countries. Basically, and in the long run, that difference is the reason why the slaves of the United States of North America (in the Black Belt) developed toward nationhood and a national movement.

Let us examine the political and military conditions that existed at the end of the Civil War. In President Johnson, who became president in 1865 after Lincoln's assassination, the landlord planters had a firm ally. At his invitation, scores of former Southern members of the House of Representatives and the Senate showed up to reclaim their seats in Congress. Had they succeeded, the political battle would have been decisively won by the Confederacy. Johnson forbade the moves by some democratic generals to implement the military victory of the North. He removed all Negro military organizations from the South and allowed the re-grouping of military organizations of the Confederacy. These military battalions roamed the countryside, pillaging, looting and murdering the Negro people. One of many examples was the Hamburg, South Carolina Massacre. There, a military unit in civilian dress, commanded by General Butler, received cannon and heavy weapons from the Federal arsenal at Augusta, Georgia. With these weapons Butler conducted the massacre at Hamburg as well as pillaging and looting throughout South Carolina.(3)

In a real sense, the planter-landlords never lost military supremacy in the South. After the defeat of the Confederacy in conventional warfare, the armed struggle assumed other forms. One of these forms was the Ku Klux Klan. The KKK, as it is called, carried out widespread intimidation of the masses. The KKK combined with other terrorist extra-legal organizations, and the Confederate military units were the forerunners of Hitler's Brown Shirts and Storm Troopers, with exactly the same division of labor. General Sheridan estimated that 3,500 Negroes were killed in the first decade after "emancipation." Other estimates range up to 10,000 the first year. At any rate, the truth is that these armed bands and military units roamed the countryside, surrounding encampments of Negroes and carrying out orgies of hangings, burnings at the stake, whippings and all manner of torture and mass murder. Throughout the South "race riots" were instigated that left whole sections of villages and towns burned and thousands of Negroes dead from mob violence. Clearly, the Negro people were being driven back into slavery. The sheer horror and violence of this first stage of the counter-revolution was a blood-soaked testament of the great democratic upsurge of the Negro and poor Anglo-American masses.

The massed conventional armies of the Confederacy were clearly defeated in the field. The surrender of General Lee at Appomattox was the formal recognition of this fact. War, however, is the extension of politics by other means and there is much in history to show that winning the military victory in no way assures the political ends. Actually, the specific property relations in the North and the South put the victorious Northern bourgeoisie in a difficult position. On the one hand, they did not dare disturb the capitalist property relations of the South; on the other hand, they had to break the political power of the landlord-planters who still dominated the Judicial branch of the government through the Supreme Court, whose justices were appointed by pre-war presidents who represented and were loyal to the slave power.

Through President Johnson, who remained loyal to the former slave owners, the slave power also continued to dominate the Executive branch. The decisive fight was being made in the Legislative branch. The landlord-planters of the South were making a strong effort to take over the House of Representatives and the Senate. This was feasible because the voting restrictions of the South allowed only pro-landlord votes to be cast; the Negroes and the vast majority of the poor Anglo-Americans were not allowed to vote. By the beginning of 1869 it was clear that the planters were winning the political battle against the financial capitalists of the North.

As a result, the financial capitalists of the North raised the battle cry of "the revolution is in danger." In response to this call stepped forward the petty bourgeois radicals. The political leadership of the revolution slipped into their hands. The best representatives of these latter-day Robespierres were Thaddeus Stevens, Frederick Douglass, Charles Sumner and Wendel Phillips. These radical democrats had the decisive task of enfranchising the freedmen so that the Southern political base, represented by pro-landlord votes, would be denied the landlords. It was this need to crush the political resistance of the landlord-planters, and this alone, that dictated the period of reconstruction.

For the moment, the needs of the Northern financial capitalists and the needs of the Negro people to some extent coincided. The Negro people and the poor Anglo-Americans of the South became pawns in what has been named the "Battle for Democracy." In fact, it was a war where the rules were heads I win, tails you lose. The Northern financial capitalists had shown their "democratic" colors by smashing unions, maintaining a 12- to 18-hour work day and by ruthlessly exploiting the labor of women and children. There was nothing in the make-up of the class to indicate that they were willing to grant the Negroes privileges that they denied the Anglo-Americans. So the Negro and Anglo-American pawns were moved forward. No matter who won the "Battle for Democracy," for sure the Negroes were going to lose. What the revisionists Foster, Dennis, Aptheker and others describe as the "Battle for Democracy" was the political phase of the struggle between the financial capitalists of the North and the blood-sucking feudal-minded landlords of the South—both capitalists—different wings of the same brutal class. At any rate, the Republicans of the North had to win over the freedmen and it was only their political opportunism that dictated the passage of the 13th and 14th Amendments to the Constitution. These amendments prohibited slavery and at least formalized the civil rights of the freedmen.

The Negro People and Reconstruction

The passage of the 13th Amendment to the Constitution (Dec. 18, 1865) abolished slavery and was the opening gun in the battle to reconstruct the South. The forces of the landlord-planters lashed out in a brutal effort to terrorize the ex-slaves and drive them back into slavery. This sharp and bitter class struggle presented the Negro masses with their first opportunity and necessity for organization. This resistance movement was known as the Negro People's Convention Movement. This movement only lasted from 1865 through 1866. However, it was organized in all states and was very important in blunting the counter-revolutionary efforts of the landlord-planters.

The 13th Amendment unleashed social forces that the Northern capitalists feared more than they feared the planters. This was shown in the way they dealt with the freedmen when they went "too far." When property rights were at stake, the Northern finance capitalists and the Southern planters found common cause.

The freed Negroes, knowing that real freedom lay only in their ownership of the land, launched a powerful movement for redistribution of the former slave holder lands. In the same manner as the present-day Brazilian, Indian or Peruvian peasant, the freedmen simply squatted on the plantations and took possession in fact. The "benefactors" of the Negro people in Washington did not hesitate to send troops to murder the squatters wherever the KKK was not up to the task of removing them. These instances exposed the real intent of the Northern capitalists. Following these "excesses" of the revolutionary Negro people, the inevitable link-up of the Northern monopolies and the remnants of the Southern landlord-planters took place. This was foretold in a letter from Engels to Marx when he wrote:

> And shall guerrillas come forth on the terrain? I certainly expect that after the definite dissolution of the armies the white trash of the South will attempt something of the sort, but I am too firmly convinced of the bourgeois nature of the planters to doubt for a moment that this will make them rabid Union men forthwith. The former are bound to attempt this with brigandage, and the planters will everywhere receive the Yankees with open arms.
>
> This business [the burning of New Orleans, Ed.] must necessarily bring the split between the planters and merchants, on the one side, and the white trash, on the other, to a head and therewith the secession is undone.(4)

This link-up between the remnants of the capitalist landlord-planters and the Northern bourgeoisie was formalized in the Hayes-Tilden Agreement of 1877.

It must be stated at this point that W. Z. Foster, on p. 337 of his book *The Negro People in American History,* concedes the point that the planters were "bourgeois." However, he fails to explain why it is that the CPUSA's program concerning the struggle for democracy in the South is based on the destruction of lingering *feudal relations,* and not feudal-like social relations, but feudal economic relations. The CPUSA fails to distinguish between the Negro people, who were developed as a people prior to the Civil War, and the Negro national movement which developed only after the defeat of Reconstruction. The leadership of the CPUSA knows full well that to admit that slavery in the United States of North America was a crude and brutal form of capitalism would bring the CPUSA's house of revisionist cards down around their heads. Therefore, they blandly state a fact and then completely disregard it.

The passage of the 14th Amendment to the Constitution, which gave large numbers of ex-slaves the right to vote, threw the masses of Negro people into the political arena. Literally thousands of Anglo-Americans (the Carpetbaggers) flooded into the South. They came with various intentions, but the basic reason for the recruitment of these missionaries was to assist the Negro people in organizing themselves as a political force and taking their indispensable place in the struggle to smash the political power of the landlord-planters.

This struggle for reconstruction gave birth to the Populist movement. As was stated above, the Northern finance capitalists were faced with the delicate task of defeating the enemy politically without disturbing the existing capitalist property relations. They found the answer in the Populist movement. Here, "poor" people were thrown into struggle against "rich" people without any consideration as to class and history. Thus a political front was skillfully built that threw the energies of the ex-slaves, poor Anglo-Americans and free Negroes against the existing power of the landlords.

From 1865-1874 the most important and powerful organization of the mass movement was the famous Union Leagues. These adjuncts of the Republican Party were often armed defense units of the ex-slaves and poor Anglo-Americans. The Negro locals of the Union Leagues were finally crushed by KKK terror in 1874.

During the period of Reconstruction a rapid urbanization of the Negro people took place. During the 1870's the Colored National Labor Union expanded until it had locals in 23 states. The CNLU associated itself with the International Workingman's Association led by Karl Marx.

One of the most powerful and broad organizations of the Populist movement was the Southern Farmers Alliance. The development of the Southern Farmers Alliance was largely independent of the integrated democratic National Farmers Alliance. The Southern Alliance (a base of the Populist Movement) endorsed white supremacy and excluded Negroes from its ranks. The role of the Alliance was to be the main battering ram to finish off the landlord-planters. The monopolies certainly intended that the Negroes were not to play a role in it. However, in the course of the political struggle with the planters, it became evident that the Alliance would have to broaden its social base in order to out fight and outvote the landlords. It was for this reason alone that the leadership of the Alliance defended the Negroes right to vote, and on many occasions, led armed men to prevent the lynching of a Negro member.

This movement was widely supported by the Negro people despite its white supremacy. In the struggle of the Alliance we can see the crucial position of the Negro masses. While the Anglo-American locals tried to dominate and dictate to the Negro locals, the Anglo-Americans were compelled to fight for the right to vote and the right to organize for the Negroes. It had been obvious from the beginning that the bourgeoisie would have to rely on the Negroes whether in organizing a struggle for progress or to exploit the wealth of the Southern region. The monopolies, acting through the Populist movement, were able to drive the planters to the wall and defeat them only by relying on the deep democratic aspirations of the Southern Negroes.

The Defeat of Reconstruction and Populism, the Imperialist Offensive and the Rise of Fascism

By the early 1870's the basic goals of the Northern capitalists had been achieved. Woodward points out in his *Origins of the New South,* "At least half of the planters after 1870 were either Northern men or organized in corporations and financed by banks." Further, "not one third of the cotton plantations of the Mississippi Valley were owned by the men who held them at the end of the war."(5) It was plain that the financial capitalists of the North had finally achieved hegemony throughout the USNA.

As the positions of the finance capitalists were consolidated, the horror of the Ku Klux Klan, now under the direction of Wall Street, was unleashed against the Negro people. For example, in Vicksburg, Mississippi, over 200 Negroes were killed in the week before the city election. President Grant reported to the Senate in 1875, "A butchery of citizens was committed at Colfax, Louisiana, which in blood thirstiness and barbarity is hardly surpassed by any acts of savage warfare."

The counter-revolution took on the aspects of the slaughter of a people. In 1871, in the area around New Orleans, 297 Negroes were lynched in one month. Reporting on the situation in North Carolina, Judge Albion W. Tourgee said, "Of the slain there were enough to furnish a battlefield and all from these three classes, the Negro, the Scalawag and the Carpetbagger.... the wounded in this silent warfare were more thousands than those who groaned upon the slopes of Gettysburg."(6)

It is worth noting that it was during the most bloody years of the terror and counter-revolution that the Republican Party increased its strength. In 1872, Grant was re-elected. The Senate held 49 Republicans against 19 Democrats; the House of Representatives held 195 Republicans against 88 Democrats.

So we see that the condition for the defeat of Reconstruction was the consolidation of the hegemony, both economic and political, of finance capital. This does not at all jibe with the CPUSA's contention that the defeat of Reconstruction was based on an agreement between the feudal landlord planters and the Northern industrialists.

The Hayes-Tilden Agreement

The presidential balloting of 1876 gave the Northern monopolies their chance to crush the last vestiges of democracy in the South while at the same time relieving themselves of any responsibility for the slaughter, new slavery (peonage) and colonization of the Negro people. Hayes, the Republican candidate, lost the popular vote by 252,224 votes to the Democrat Tilden who, without the demagogy of Hayes, represented strictly the planters. Tilden claimed the election. The Republicans challenged the ballots from South Carolina, Florida, Louisiana and Oregon. This maneuver threw Tilden out of the race but still left Hayes one electoral vote short of the needed majority. A constitutional crisis followed. There were many threats and even a phony plan for the Southern Tilden supporters to take Washington by a coup d'état. Of course, the crisis and the threats of a new civil war were merely the smokescreen for a legal coup. This came in the form of the infamous Hayes-Tilden Agreement. Basically, the Agreement was to turn the Southern state governments where the Republicans still held democratic populist control (including the governments of South Carolina and Louisiana) over to the Democrats. The most telling part of the Agreement was that the North would withdraw all Federal troops from the South and let the

South settle its own problems. By returning the state governments to the Democratic Party, now fully controlled by the imperialists, and by deepening the concept of states' rights, counter-revolution would triumph and the democratic masses of the North would be legally blocked.

The Hayes-Tilden Agreement had the same effect in the South as when President Hindenburg of Germany "felt" compelled to appoint Adolph Hitler as Chancellor of Germany. Every fascist current in the South zeroed in on the Negro masses and the democratically minded poor Anglo-Americans.

The Fascist Offensive

The Hayes-Tilden Agreement and the following withdrawal of Federal troops from the South in 1877 was only a big event in a well defined trend. To the degree that the financial capitalists politically subdued the landlord-planters, to that degree did the monopolies hand the Negroes back into a new slavery. As the troops left, the landlords surfaced as a political power. However, this time they were not in opposition to but were the direct and brutal agents of the blood-thirsty monopolies. It became clear that they had never lost military supremacy over the Negro people. At no time and at no place had the Negroes ever won a clear political majority. The pro-slavery storm troops, allied with the terrorist KKK, never allowed Reconstruction to stabilize or develop.

In the South, the offensive of imperialism had a marked fascist character. The withdrawal of the Federal troops was the signal for the "revolt of the poor whites."

The democratic, anti-monopoly Populist movement reached its high point just before the counter-revolution. In the South the Populist movement was led by such men as Ben Tillman and Tom Watson. These so-called leaders were opportunist vacillating men who constantly compromised with the landlords while trying to fight them. The most crucial and decisive question was the question of the unity of the Negro and Anglo-American masses. Despite all the speeches to the contrary, Watson, Tillman, et. al., never moved to do away with Negro segregation in the Farmers Alliance. The only outcome of a revolutionary mass movement led by vacillating, petty bourgeois leaders was the fascist drive.

Just as the Populist movement was led by Tillman and Company, when the monopolies needed to crush the landlords, so the "revolt of the poor whites" was also led by Tillman and Company when there was the need to crush Populism and especially the Negro masses.

The newly enfranchised poor Anglo-Americans from the hills, who were maneuvered out of the struggle between the monopolies and the landlords, were imbued with rabid white supremacy and turned against the Negro masses. There was no "revolt of the poor whites" any more than there was a Hitler-inspired revolt of the poor peasant or the lumpen-proletariat. What took place at the birth of imperialism and fascism was a skillful maneuver which relied on the centuries old white supremacy to co-opt the Populist movement, garb it in the mantle of the Ku Klux Klan and push it onto the stage of history as the hangman of democracy.

This "revolt of the poor whites" was led by such fascists as Vardman, Tillman and Cole Blase. They constructed a social order that was faithfully copied by Hitler, who also referred to his fascist movement as the "revolt of the poor peasants," "the petty bourgeoisie," etc. In the pamphlet "The Economics of Barbarism"(7) Kuczynski and Witt point out how the rules for Hitler's Slave State were copied from the black codes.

Some of the fascist characteristics of the counter-revolution were: (1) It conformed to the description of being the "open terrorist dictatorship of the most reactionary, most chauvinistic and most imperialist elements of finance capital." (2) "The accession to power of fascism is not an ordinary succession of one bourgeois government by another, but a substitution of one state form of class domination of the bourgeoisie — bourgeois democracy, for another form — open terrorist dictatorship." (3) "Fascism comes to power as a party of attack on the revolutionary movement of the proletariat, on the masses of the people who are in a state of unrest; yet it stages its accession to power as a revolutionary movement against the bourgeoisie on behalf of the whole nation."(8)

What made up the fascist character of the counter-revolution was not simply its brutality or violence, but the fact that the "revolt of the poor whites" cloaked itself in the mantle of saving the South. The fascist-led "revolt" was the absolute agent of finance capital of the North. The counter-revolution attacked and overthrew the Reconstruction bourgeois democratic governments. Then, the fascists substituted a reign of terror as the new state form of domination over the emerging Negro Nation. In the Anglo-American Nation the capitalists in the main relied on deception, bribery and fraud; in short, on bourgeois democracy. This was not the case in the Black Belt! Here, the rule of finance capital was maintained by an unheard of reign of terror, legal and extra-legal, both by police and the KKK.

From time to time Communists have raised this question of fascism in the Negro Nation and in the entire South only to retract their statements because they held that there was a contradiction between their conception of fascism and imperialism. So they were told, and so they thought. Fascism is rampant imperialism. George Seldes was quite correct when he said that fascism is imperialism turned inward. To understand the rise of fascism in the South means taking fully into account that, even during the periods of radical reconstruction, segregation remained a way of life. In the Union Leagues, in the Labor Unions, in the Farmers Alliance, there were Anglo-American and Negro locals. Because the decisive element of Negro Anglo-American unity was not fought for, it was easy for the fascists to appear on the scene as the progressive leaders of the "poor whites." Confusion around this question of the role of the Anglo-American leaders has been common.

For example, in Foster's book *The Negro People in American History,* on p. 381, he states "Ben Tillman of Georgia [actually Tillman was from South Carolina, Ed.] declared for Negro, white cooperation..." and "Pitchfork Tillman, a rabid white chauvinist..." (Foster's book is marked by such contradictions. It would seem that the book was written by several people who didn't speak to one another or that Foster had a severely split personality.) Foster accounts for the transition of Tillman and Watson from democrats and chauvinists in this manner: "In the early upswing of the Alliance movement, they scoffed at the boogey of 'white supremacy,' made fiery attacks on the big planters, and expressed solidarity with the oppressed Negro masses. Unstable petty bourgeois elements, however, they all wound up as the most vicious of Negro baiters'."(9)

This is a typical example of Foster's historiography: subjective, inaccurate and an affront to Marxism. According to this sort of analysis, Benito Mussolini, a Socialist who wrote to Lenin and marched on Rome under the banner of the Dictatorship of the Proletariat, introduced fascism in Italy because he was an "unstable petty bourgeois element" who wound up as the most "vicious" of anti-communists. With the same analysis German fascism can be explained because Hitler was a petty bourgeois element. No, Mr.

Bourgeois, this will never do; we have to look deeper, something the Communist Party dared not do. Any investigation shows that the Watsons, Tillmans, etc., were elements that were groomed and paid for by the finance capitalists. When it was necessary to organize the masses to gain the political victory over the landlords, these "leaders" came forth with a particular line; then, when it was necessary to stop the democratic upsurge, prevent it from getting out of hand, they took another line. Yet, Foster's line inevitably leads to the conclusion that the white chauvinist textbooks are correct, that the counter-revolution was a reaction to "black reconstruction." The facts show otherwise— the "revolt of the poor whites" was merely the mask for the fascist counter-revolution financed and conducted by Northern finance capital.

A political force, constructed and funded by finance capital, which overthrows a legal bourgeois democratic government and substitutes as a state form the open terrorist dictatorship of the most reactionary, most chauvinistic elements of finance capital is called fascist. Such a political state we call *fascism.*

It should be noted that one element of the historic roots of the Communist Party goes through the old Socialist Party into the Populist movement. The Populist concepts are still strong in the CPUSA. Their "anti-monopoly coalition" is but one of these Populist slogans, if not the most important. It must be said that the main reason for the confusion of the Communist Party on this period of Reconstruction is the fact that they themselves are populists and syndicalists, not Marxist-Leninists.

Many of the Populist leaders, such as Ben Tillman, who became the worst white chauvinists and fascists, were "progressive" leaders of the mass movement. Like their followers, Hitler and Mussolini, these fascist leaders of the South were recruited from the people's movement. This was the only way that fascism could have the necessity social base.

The positive aspects of the Populist movement were proof enough that the general toiling masses cannot move forward without the Negro people. This history also shows that the special democratic demands of the Negro people cannot help but be the demand for political independence.

As the heavy hand of imperialism was clamped on the South, and especially on the Black Belt, the mass movement became a real Negro movement. Its main content was the special demand of the Negro people for anti-lynch laws and for civil rights. Prior to the defeat of Reconstruction, the demands of the Negro people for bread, land and liberty were so intertwined with the demands of the general toiling masses that to separate the motion of the Negro people from the rest of the toiling masses in the Black Belt was impossible.

Even during the worst days of reaction, it was impossible to totally single out the Negro for the chain gang, the lynch rope, the burning stake or the peonage camp.

The terrorist military overthrow of Reconstruction opened the way for the re-enslavement of the Negro people. The peonage system, the shares farming system and the black codes forced this re-enslavement. At the same time the forced segregation laid the basis for the development of a Negro bourgeoisie. Existing insurance companies refused to do business with Negroes, so Negro insurance companies arose. Existing banks refused to service Negroes, so a Negro banking system arose. The old axiom of "Whatever can happen will" was proven in the development of the Negro bourgeoisie. The dialectics of reaction transformed the enslavement of the Africans into the enslavement of a nation.

The Negro Bourgeois Democratic National Movement

The nature of the struggle of the Negro people changed rapidly during Reconstruction, and the counter-revolution accelerated this change. What began as the struggle of a landless peasant mass with a minute urban proletariat rapidly became the struggle of an oppressed nation with all classes developing rapidly under the pressures of fascist imperialism.

Under such circumstances the developing Negro bourgeoisie split in two. That portion which sold to the people and therefore had to rely on the people came out in opposition to Wall Street imperialism. The portion that sold to the imperialists and therefore had to rely on the imperialists became the Negro people's comprador bourgeoisie. Woodson and Wesley noted this split in the Negro leadership:

> Other Negroes who thoroughly understand the inevitable result from such surrender gave up the fight for democracy in return for the profits of segregation. The extension work of church organizations, social welfare agencies and institutions of learning controlled by white advocates of

caste have all been brought under the direction of Negroes who have sealed their lips as to actual democracy. Such Negroes are approached beforehand and thoroughly tested as to their stand on race matters. If they conform to the requirements of genuflecting Toadyism they are placed in these commanding positions to use their influence in keeping the Negro content with their lot.(10)

The base of the Negro comprador bourgeoisie is still the clergy, social welfare agencies, the educational bureaucracy, and the governmental and political bureaucracy. It was from this split in the bourgeoisie that the Negro People's National Liberation Movement arose.

The struggle of the Negro masses was directed first against slavery and then against peonage. Such a movement could not and was not simply a "Negro" movement except in the sense of its being national. During the period of the overthrow of Reconstruction, the struggle of the Negro masses could not be separated from the struggle of the rest of the colonial world. In fact, the struggle of the Negro masses against imperialism was an integral part of the struggle of the Cubans, the Puerto Ricans, the peoples of Santo Domingo, Haiti, the Philippines and everywhere that USNA imperialism was enslaving nations and peoples. Neither could the light for the Negro people be separated from the struggle of the workers and dirt farmers against the Robber Baron monopolies.

The Negro people protested the imperialist acquisition of Haiti, the Virgin Islands and the West Indies. Not only did they fight against the practice of color discrimination, they clearly saw that their fight for democracy and equality was undercut by the expansion of imperialism.

Both Presidents Harding and Coolidge were compelled to appoint Negro Commissions to look into conditions in the newly conquered territories. These commissions could not accomplish anything, but they were evidence of the international concern of the growing Negro national bourgeoisie.

The Church

The Negro church emerged from slavery as the only social institution allowed first by the slave masters and then the Wall Street masters of the South. The leading role of the Negro church remains stamped on the movement to this day. Consequently, in the beginning at least, spokesmen for both sections of the new Negro bourgeoisie spoke from the pulpit. The result of this was that the movement was split into various locales and, therefore, individual leaders instead of masses seemed to emerge as the leading factor. This was especially true because the churches did not exist in limbo. They were, in fact, governed by bourgeois clerics in the North and sometimes the metropolitan South. Furthermore, the leading bishops and other church officials were an integral part of the Anglo-American ruling class. The "Negro church" is a misnomer. In fact, "Negro churches" are Anglo-American capitalist-controlled churches for Negroes. At one time the Colored Baptist and the AME Zion Churches made a stiff fight for their independence, but such a fight could not be won under capitalism. The only exception to the fact that Anglo-American bourgeois clerics dominate the Negro church is the innumerable store-front churches.

Some of the churches under slavery became important and wealthy institutions. After the capture of Atlanta, General Sherman called together the leading slaves and free Negroes and was surprised to find that one slave-owned church was valued at $50,000 and another at $35,000.(11)

Although the slaves had been taught the European religions in an effort to pacify and ideologically chain them, the church also served as a meeting place to plot escapes and plan such resistance as was possible under the conditions of slavery.

During the counter-revolution there was a great demand for segregated churches and when that didn't seem to be enough, there was the demand for entirely separated church administration systems. This experiment in apartheid was set aside when it was realized that such a complete separation would mean Negro bishops and a church attuned to the problems of the Negro people. The church rulers soon saw the folly of abandoning religious thought to the Negroes as the Southern churches had done after the Civil War(12). Thus the church remained a Trojan horse to the Negro movement, populated by Negroes and controlled by a bourgeois Anglo-American clergy. It could not but play a dual role, both progressive and reactionary. The major aspect, however, was to drain off the militant energy of the Negro people. The fact that the Negro church, despite its anti-democratic structure, became the birthplace of so many Negro movements is a testimony to both the vitality of the

Negro masses' democratic aspirations and the deeply rooted social position of this institution.

The Split in the Negro Movement

Booker T. Washington's famous Atlanta speech signaled the fully matured split in the Negro National Movement. Washington became the most powerful and tyrannical Negro individual in the movement. A word from Washington was enough to financially and politically destroy almost anyone who dared oppose him. In his position of directing the funds that went to social service agencies and to the schools, it was simple to transform that economic position into a political one. His position was an extension of the "Head Negro" under slavery. Washington's Atlanta speech of 1895 was a high-sounding declaration of compromise and acceptance of the social and economic enslavement of the Negro people. Washington's statement that "the wisest among my race understand that the agitation of questions of social equality is the extremest folly" was the battle challenge to the Negro national bourgeoisie. Led by Du Bois and J. M. Trotter, they set out to organize the majority who were resisting this line of Washington's. Woodson and Wesley report: "With the exception of a small minority, the Negroes regarded this policy as a surrender to the oppressors who desired to reduce the whole race to menial service."(13)

Harry Haywood characterizes Washington as: "The voice of the embryonic middle class."(14) Foster paints him as a "bourgeois nationalist"(15). Foster and other Communist Party writers and theoreticians quite correctly characterize DuBois as a Negro bourgeois leader—pointing out that in respect to building up Negro businesses Du Bois and his followers outdid Washington in some respects. Finally, Foster makes an attempt to explain the obvious difference between these two leaders: "the main point of divergence between the movements however—and this was decisive, was where Washington preached humility and submission for the Negro people, DuBois and his followers advocated a course of militant struggle."(16)

Foster's description of the split in the Negro bourgeoisie insults the intelligence of even the most naive Marxist. Was it that Washington just happened to choose the path of submission and DuBois just happened to choose the path of struggle? Not at all. Such historiography makes history revolve around the subjective whims of leading individuals. The difference between a Congolese Lumumba and Mobuto was hardly their likes and dislikes—it was their class position in relation to imperialism—and so it was with DuBois and Washington. The maturing of a modem nation under the oppression of imperialism inevitably brings out two wings of the national bourgeoisie: on the one hand, the comprador bourgeoisie and on the other, the national bourgeoisie with the social and political and economic base that has been previously described.

Foster was an intelligent man and the Communist Party gave him a staff of Ph.D.'s to assist him in writing his book on Negro history. Why was it that the class and social differences were so incomprehensible to him? The secret of its ignorance is simply this: The Communist Party is tied by a thousand financial, social and political threads to the liberal Anglo-American bourgeoisie. These threads absolutely proscribed the Party's understanding of the Negro question as a national colonial question. Therefore, relying on the backwardness of the radicals of the USNA, the CPUSA found it possible to do away with the most glaring theoretical and social contradictions by either ignoring them or obscuring them with bourgeois drivel.

The fact is that Washington was the leader of a maturing Negro comprador bourgeoisie. DuBois emerged as a leader of the Negro national bourgeoisie. By overlooking these contradictions, the CPUSA could claim to be the Party of the Negro people. Actually, the CP represented the Negro national bourgeoisie, if anything at all. The social background of the leading Negroes in the CP shows this. To name but a few—Ben Davis, son of a leading Negro family in Atlanta, Georgia; Dr. James Jackson, Ph.D., professor, son of a leading family of South Carolina; Langston Hughes, a leading Negro author and poet. Even such outstanding non-party leaders as Eslanda Goode and her husband, Paul Robeson, could not represent anything but the radical Negro bourgeoisie. Such men as Pettis Perry, a Negro proletarian communist leader who was constantly harassed by the CPUSA leadership, never reconciled himself to the Party's revisionism. Another exception was Harry Haywood, the Negro author and sociologist who was almost outlawed from the CPUSA for publishing his *Negro Liberation.* Consistent Negro Marxist intellectuals such as Charles P. Mann were driven out of the Party for their Marxist ideals.

The fundamental difference between the position of the Com

44

Death Rather Than Slavery
Source: Langston Hughes & Milton Meltzer, A Pictorial History of the
Negro in America (New York: Crown Publishers, Inc., 1956)

munist Labor Party and the CPUSA on the Negro question is the description by the CLP of the Negro question as a modern national colonial question with all the ramifications for the proletarian revolution and the daily class struggle. The CP position on the Negro question is an abstraction that flows from the fundamental Party position that the movement in the Negro Nation is a continuation of the "Battle for Democracy" and the program must be a complete wiping out of the remains of feudalism and the completion of the bourgeois democratic revolution. Under the conditions of fascism and the total control of monopoly the CP proposals become thoroughly exposed as reactionary.

The CP position on the Negro question is not simply an isolated case. On the contrary, the CP is quite consistent. Jay Lovestone's contribution to the CP was American exceptionalism in American political economy. Browder's contribution was American exceptionalism in the critique of American imperialism. Foster's contribution was American exceptionalism on the national question in regard In the Negro Nation. His concept of a "nation within a nation" is not so striking because it is a unique concept in Marxism, but in that it is an extension of the basic form of CPUSA revisionism— American exceptionalism.

The Negro question is not an exception. Even Foster admits that " the peonage known as share cropping (much akin to types of tenancy found in colonial Asia), which (was) enforced by terror ism." The path of peoples from slavery is into peonage. This is just as true for the Negro people as for the Mexicans or the Puerto Ricans or the Hondurans. Foster admits to this when he writes, "It had been the tragic history of emancipated slaves, during the past century and throughout the western hemisphere—whether Indians or Negroes— that they did not pass from the status of slavery to that of free farmers and workers, but rather to one form of peonage or another."(19) There, apparently, the science of history ends and the development of the Negro question reverts back to the Communist Party's specific form of revisionism—American exceptionalism.

Under such intellectual giants as Dr. W.E.B. DuBois and James Monroe Trotter, editor of the *Boston Guardian,* the Negro bourgeoisie broke into the political life of the USNA. This vigorous and new bourgeoisie did not confine itself to the national scene but, understanding the necessity of fighting the enemy in the international arena, took the fight against imperialism into the World War I Peace Conference (1918). They demanded that the spread of imperialism be halted and that the African colonies and Haiti be set free. They formed political organizations such as the National Independent Political Rights League to enforce the Constitution.

It may appear that DuBois was the world-wide champion of the dark-skinned people and not necessarily fighting imperialism *per se.* But a closer examination will show that the only place for imperialism to expand was to the dark-skinned people, and the fight for color equality was the form that the anti-imperialist struggle had to take.

Because of the "race riots," lynch law, and tightening segregation, this Negro bourgeoisie enjoyed a rapid growth. The Negro as a consumer held little attraction for the expanding monopolies so the Negro market was wide open to this Negro bourgeoisie. Negro businesses doubled between 1910 and 1920. By 1920, Negro farmers owned 13,948,512 acres of land and, in addition, Negro tenants rented land valued at $1,676,315,864.(18) Where Anglo-American businesses failed to service the Negro people, Negro businesses arose in catering, personal service, drayage and storage, forging and carriage making, butchering and mattress making.

Under the leadership of DuBois, the Pan-African movement was formed. Speaking in the name of dark-skinned peoples everywhere, its aims were fighting for justice, ending the slave trade and opposing the liquor traffic. The Negro national bourgeoisie extended its base throughout the world. The internationalism of the Negro bourgeoisie exists to this day. The ringing cries for world peace from Martin Luther King and the eloquent cries for democracy and justice in the civil rights movement today are but an extension of the bourgeois movement of 70 years ago.

The right wing of the national bourgeoisie, the comprador wing, remained firmly under the control of Booker T. Washington. Little has changed with respect to the role of the comprador. It is obvious that along with the concept of Asians fighting Asians and Africans fighting Africans, there is a definite move afoot to have Negroes control Negroes. This "solution" to the Negro question is becoming more and more apparent. In 1970, 665 Negroes held elective offices in 11 southern states. By 1974 this number rose to 1307. This total includes 2 U.S. Congressmen, 60 state legislators, 622 municipal officials and 304 education officials. More Negroes have been elected to public office in the South than any other region of the United States. The biggest gains in the recent elections of 1974 came in Alabama and South Carolina. Two Negroes are sitting in the Alabama Senate for the first time, and the number of Negroes in the State House rose from 3 to 13. In South Carolina the number of Negro representatives also went from 3 to 13.

Naturally, revisionists hail these "election victories" without at all estimating that what we are witnessing is the gradual application of the politics of neo-colonialism to the Negro colony. Who can control the raging Negro movement for national liberation better than Negro compradors? The imperialist leopard has not changed its spots. Far from being a cause to rejoice and lower the guard, the massive acceptance on the part of the ruling class of elected Negro officials is cause for alarm. While we welcome and fight for the participation of broad masses of Negroes in the political life of the Negro colony, we are not going to be fooled into welcoming a gang of Negro Chiang Kai-sheks to replace the cops in the same way the cops have replaced the Ku Klux Klan as the imperialist spearhead against the Negro people.

The hegemony of the Negro national bourgeoisie began to be

consolidated in the Niagara Movement, founded by James Monroe Trotter in 1905 and headed by W.E.B. DuBois. The Niagara Movement took as its goal the full equality of the Negroes. Its weapons were to be militant in politics and propaganda. This movement, gaining wide support among the masses, founded the militant Equal Rights Leagues. Clearly, there was a danger of the Negro bourgeoisie breaking the imperialist economic and political fetters. Moving behind the Anglo-American upper-class liberals, the imperialists moved to counter this threatened breakaway. The National Association for the Advancement of Colored People (NAACP) was formed May 30, 1909. It soon absorbed the Niagara Movement and Equal Rights Leagues.

Foster states, "The basis of the new NAACP was the rising wave of resistance among the Negro people, earlier expressed by the Niagara Movement." This theory accords with the needs of the imperialists and is contradicted by Foster himself (?) in the same book, where he states, "Among the white liberals signing the call were Professor John Dewey, Jane Addams, William Dean Howells, Rabbi Emil G. Hirsh, Reverend John Haynes Holmes, Dr. Henry Moskowitz, Dr. Charles E. Parkhurst, Louis Wald, Mary E. Wolley and Susan P. Wharton. There were also several white socialists among the signers, including William English Walling, Charles Edward Russel, J.G. Philips Stokes, Mary E. Dreier, Florence Kelly and Mary Ovington."(19)

With this gang of honey-mouthed liberals fronting for the imperialists, what chance did the Negro movement have? Little wonder that a militant like J.M. Trotter refused to join the NAACP and fought to keep the Equal Rights Leagues out too.

Actually the formation of the NAACP and its co-optation of the Niagara Movement and the Equal Rights Leagues spelled the end of the independent efforts of the Negro bourgeoisie to unite against imperialism. The real basis of the NAACP was imperialism, exemplified by the backing of these imperialists—Mrs. Cyrus McCormick, Harvey Firestone, the DuPonts and the like. The policy of imperialist co-optation of the Negro people's movements has remained a prime tactic of the imperialists.

**The original leaders of the Niagara movement in 1905, with
DuBois the second from the right in the second row.**
Source: Langston Hughes & Milton Meltzer, A Pictorial History of
the Negro in America (New York: Crown Publishers, Inc., 1956)

The Negro People's National Liberation Movement
During the crisis and depression years of 1920-1922, one-half
to two-thirds of all Negro businesses were wiped out.(20) This

could not but have the most striking effect on the Negro people's movement. The budding energetic Negro national bourgeois movement was defeated by imperialism; its economic base was all but done away with. The Negro businessman was hurled down into the ranks of the Negro proletariat.

The post-1917 period saw the Negro workers begin to assert themselves in an independent manner. Prior to this period it was not possible for the Negro workers to express themselves independently of the Negro national bourgeoisie. This was not because of the weakness of the Negro workers, but since the imperialists inherited the color forms of oppression from slavery, this was the only social form at their disposal. The content of the oppression had changed from the oppression of individual slaves to the oppression of a nation. In the early 1900s, as today, the imperialists struggled to maintain this color form of oppression. Thus it appears that the central contradiction was between all "blacks" and all "whites" rather than between workers and capitalists.

Given the economic history of the USNA it is impossible for the Negro workers to march very far in advance of the general working class of the USNA. Therefore, the construction of a party of the working class became a historical necessity and inevitability. The advances the Negro workers made during the 1930's and 1940's were in the main due to the militant leadership of the Communists, particularly the Negro Communists. Proof of the growing awareness of the Negro workers and the lower middle class is expressed in the fact that in 1938 the Communist Party registered 10,500 Negro Communists.

Negro Communists played a heroic role in the building of the unions, especially the C.I.O. The role of the Negro Communists in the building of the Party in the South was indispensible. Large sections of the Negro people followed the line of the Communist Party because of the struggles led by Negro Communists and also because the most radical elements of the Negro bourgeoisie were in or openly backed the CPUSA.

Because the CPUSA played an important role in the Negro people's national liberation movement, the betrayals of the Negro people by the CP had a particularly destructive effect. The first of these was the dissolution of the CP in 1944. The second main betrayal was the unconstitutional dissolution of the Party in the South in 1949. This betrayal was accompanied by the wrecking of the

Following the bombing of their home in Birmingham, Alabama in 1956, Rev. Shuttlesworth escorts his children to school after State Troopers were called to open the school, but refused to admit black students who tried to enroll.
Source: Ebony Magazine, Vol. 24, No. 10, August, 1971, "The South Today"

Marchers hold hands during demonstration as firemen spray them with firehoses.
Source: Ebony Magazine, Vol. 24, No. 10, August, 1971, "The South Today"

powerful Negro Labor Councils. Since the most advanced Negro workers were in or close to the Party, these anti-working class actions had an especially destructive effect on the general Negro people's national liberation movement. The movement floundered momentarily, the leadership either totally disoriented, scared off or bought off.

It was under such conditions that the magnificent struggle in Montgomery, Alabama, broke out on December 4, 1955. The militant bravery, the ingenuity and steadfastness of the Negro people in Montgomery was a catalyst to reactivate broad sections of the Negro people and consequently broad sections of the petty bourgeois "left." The struggle in Montgomery also brought about a reawakening of interest in revolutionary Marxism. The Montgomery Boycott awakened the new militant black student movement, and that movement was the political base for the S.D.S. In a real and concrete way, the rebirth of the Negro people's national liberation movement caused the revitalization of the revolutionary movement in the USNA.

During the massive struggle of the Negro people in Birmingham in the spring of 1963, it became evident that there was a new internal contradiction developing. That development was the fight of the Negro proletariat for its independent role and the leadership of the Negro masses. Despite the ruthless police repression and the betrayal of the so-called leadership, a new stage in the struggle was evolving. This emerging stage became more pronounced during the summer of 1964. In Harlem, Bedford-Stuyvesant and Rochester, the Negro national minority workers fully rejected the petty bourgeois leaders. The history of the mass struggle of the Negro people was taking a new turn. In Watts, on August 11, 1965, this new stage— this new qualitative development—reached maturity. Not simply rejecting but shooting the mis-leaders, the Negro national minority workers were hurled face-to-face against the naked power of the state.

Under these conditions of revolutionary mass struggle, the revisionism of the CPUSA became fully exposed. Acting as the left-flank guard of President Lyndon Johnson, the Editors of *Political Affairs* moaned advice, "What is essential of course, is the mounting of a real war against poverty."(21)

The revolutionary Uncle Tom, William C. Taylor summed up

Fireman assists Policeman in arrest of demonstrator in 1963.
Source: Ebony Magazine, Vol. 24, No. 10, August, 1971,
"The South Today"

the cause and effect of the Watts uprising, "Can anyone doubt that
Chief Parker's racist statements helped to pave the way for the infil-
tration of the Los Angeles police department by Birchites and ultra-
Right elements to the detriment of the impartial enforcement of law
and order."(22) Begging for the re-establishment of the bourgeoisie's hegemony over the struggle, Taylor concluded, "Within the
Negro community there has developed a higher and stronger level
of unity than ever before. This development has grown out of the
recognition of the Negro middle class of their responsibility in relation to the aspirations of the poor and working Negro people."
Aptheker topped it all off by his cry for the Red Cross to investigate
the jails that were crammed with Negro national minority fighters.

The Watts uprising objectively linked the struggle of the Anglo-
American workers to the national liberation movement in the Negro
Nation. The new level of struggle that matured in Watts was carried
even further by the Detroit uprising of 1967. There the participation
of Southern Anglo-American workers from the Negro Nation was,
for the ruling class, a terrible harbinger of the future. Detroit
showed that the struggle not only linked the Anglo-American work-

**Demonstrators are attacked by police dog during protest
march in Birmingham, 1963, as they sought to integrate
public facilities.**
Source: Ebony Magazine, Vol. 24, No. 10, August, 1971,
"The South Today"

ing class to the Negro national liberation struggles, but through the
Negro national liberation movement to the whole of the colonial
world. Indeed, the Negro people, whose enslavement was so necessary to the growth of capitalism, were completing the encirclement
of imperialism of the USNA and shaking it to its foundations.

The Negro workers, who have now arisen in all their splendid
heroism, had to cast aside non-violence as a tactic. They had to
move directly into a confrontation with the state. In making this
confrontation, the Negro national liberation movement completed
the ground work for an international front of struggle against
imperialism.

There can be no doubt that under the hegemony of the Negro workers the whole national liberation movement will leap forward. The imperialists know this better than we do. This is the reason that they will pay any price to keep the movement in the hands of the non-violent elements—that is, in the hands of the compromised petty bourgeoisie. One of the major aspects of this tactic is to revive and rearm the petty bourgeois, compromised, syndicalist, populist Communist Party of the United States of America and their assistants.

During this period the government took what appeared to be a contradictory position. On the one hand the government was getting ever more deeply committed to the genocidal criminal imperialist war in Vietnam. Both the Kennedy and Eisenhower administrations, while nakedly building, funding and supporting the fascist neo-colonial regimes, came out more and more with court decisions and the use of Federal troops in support of the "constitutional rights" of the Negro people.

A close examination of the facts will show that the contradiction was more apparent than real. If we view the policy of USNA imperialism during this period from the broad historical point of view, we have to conclude that USNA imperialism did not oppose the breakaway of the colonial masses from direct colonial oppression. Quite to the contrary, there was considerable overt and invert assistance. This activity, directed by the CIA through the colonial elite had as its purpose the transition from the direct colonial system to the system of neo-colonialism. The reason for this was the economic reality that the direct colonial system favored the financier of the specific imperialist country that occupied the colony. But the neo-colony, because it has a national state, is consequently open to USNA and transnational financial capital.

The history of the decade of the 1960's is the history of assassinations of popular leaders, of intrigue, subversion and the unleashing of the horrors of USNA military might against any patriotic force that attempted to guide the anti-colonial revolution onto the path of real independence, that is, to socialism.

The USNA imperialists very well understood and understand that a powerful wave of national liberation struggles would be the inevitable result of the liberation of China and the defeat of the imperialists in Korea. As has happened before in history, the CIA was called into action to utilize the revolutionary spirit and self-sacrifice of the masses for their own ends. History will record how the blood of hundreds of thousands of African and Asian freedom fighters was utilized by USNA and transnational capital for the historic defeat of direct colonialism and the consolidation of neo-colonialism and its chief sponsor—USNA financial imperialism.

The truth, shown by these facts, is that the USNA imperialists were perfectly willing to shift their political tactics to conform to the changing economic situation. Again the guidelines were, "no permanent friends, only permanent interests."

This truth also emerged from the approach of the government to the Negro people's national liberation movement.

Ever since the recession of 1948 there has been an increasing flight of industry from the North to the South. The reasons for this were the great quantities of fresh water, raw materials and the unorganized, hard working, poverty-stricken labor force that resided in the South. However, it soon became clear that it would be impossible to fully exploit the labor in the South so long as the law—written and unwritten—effectively kept the Negro out of industry. Thus, there unfolded a second edition of the tragedy of reconstruction. The moral force, the physical energy, the democratic aspirations of the Negro people were cynically directed by the Kennedy and Johnson administrations to achieve the goals of the financiers. That goal was to create the legal and social conditions to proletarianize the Negro. One by one the laws of segregation were struck down. Also struck down were the scores of Negro leaders who understood the trap into which the Negro movement was being led. No one can doubt the economic and social advance of a large section of the Negro people as a result of the movement of the 1960's. But the historic result was the drawing into industry and industrial exploitation of the millions of Negro toilers who heretofore had been excluded from the industrial life of the South.

To complete the picture it should be clear that the Wall Street rulers of the South do not need laws to enforce segregation. The most liberal northern city testifies to this. On the other hand, our historical examples show us that while the designs of the capitalists for the South cannot be achieved without arousing the deep democratic aspirations of the Negro people, the imperialists never allow these aspirations and the movement to get out of hand. Once the desired goals are achieved, the imperialists unleash an extra-legal terror to prevent the movement from going too far. The dramatic resurgence of the Ku Klux Klan and the other fascist movements testify that the reaction is now underway.

There can be no question that the Negro people's national liberation movement (including the movement of the Negro national minority workers) has opened the gates of the Socialist revolution. The Negro workers to the extent that they occupy the strategic position of the unskilled basic workers will radicalize the majority of the working class. In order to attack the Negro workers, the government is going to have to attack and become entangled with the majority of the working class. The position of the Negro workers is strategic and they will not fail. History will record the stirring of the Negro proletariat as the beginning of the American Socialist revolution. In this historic truth is the fundamental significance of the task of constructing a Marxist-Leninist Communist Party. The only course for revolutionaries today is to link the struggle of the Negro masses to the difficult task of building and strengthening such a Party. The Negro movement has been a catalyst to re-activate the whole objective process of the revolution. That task can be completed only by consolidating the Marxist-Leninist conscious expression of the subconscious revolutionary process.

CHAPTER FOUR

NATIONAL EVOLUTION AND THE NEGRO NATION

History shows that nations did not always exist. Society travelled a long and complicated road of development before nations appeared.

A nation is not merely a historical category but a historical category belonging to a definite epoch, the epoch of rising capitalism. The process of elimination of feudalism and the development of capitalism is at the same time a process of the constitution of people into nations.(1)

In the formation of nations, the bourgeoisie played the leading role. The chief problem for a young bourgeoisie is the problem of the market. Its aim is to sell its goods and to emerge victorious from competition with the bourgeoisie of another nationality. Hence, its desire to secure its "own," its "home" market. "The market is the first school in which the bourgeoisie learns its nationalism."(2) With the "discovery" of the "new world," mass migrations, forced and voluntary, involving millions of people of different colors, languages and customs, took place. These immigrants, along with the native Indian peoples, were basic productive forces that laid the basis for new nations to be formed.

The nations that exist today in the Western Hemisphere have travelled a long road since their wars of national liberation. The nations of Mexico, Brazil, and Anglo-America all waged wars against I the Spanish, Portuguese and English colonial governments, respectively. These revolutionary wars of independence were led by the rising young bourgeoisie of these new nations.

In the stage of imperialism nations are also formed. Imperialism forces divergent people together; it compels them to take a common language, usually the language of the imperialists; to develop a common economic life; and to live in a common territory. For example, African countries had their boundaries drawn by Britain, France, Belgium, Germany, and the imperialists of the USNA as they struggled for and divided the spoils among themselves. Members of the same tribes found themselves belonging to different countries due to arbitrary lines drawn on maps. As time passed, these peoples came to consider themselves members of particular nations rather than members of a particular tribe. In the stage of capitalist imperialism, the leading role in the struggle for national liberation has to be played by the working class of that nation. The tiny bourgeoisie is too weak, too compromised and too tied to property to effectively struggle against imperialism. The days of the bourgeoisie leading the struggle for national liberation are long over. It can be seen from the example of Algeria that unless the working class is in the lead of the national liberation struggle the most that can be achieved is a neo-colonial status.

The majority of the non-sovereign nations are under the economic control of USNA imperialism. The three nations under the direct economic and political control of USNA imperialism are Puerto Rico, the Negro Nation and the Philippines. The national liberation of these oppressed nations will not be on the order of the previous bourgeois revolutions. These national liberation struggles will be led by the proletariat, with political independence and socialism as the only and necessary aim.

In the USNA the main question facing any revolutionary party is whether it understands the role of the Negro people. Most parties and groupings in the USNA evaluate the Negro people either as one homogeneous mass of "lumpen-proletariat" or all "Black workers" suffering from "racism." The CPUSA leads the pack in distorting the historical development of the Negro Nation. Their evaluation of the oppression of the Negro people ranges from either denying the existence of the Negro Nation altogether and naming the source as individual subjective "racism" in the hearts and minds of "white" workers to saying that the root of the oppression is due to the "incompletion of the bourgeois revolution" in the Black Belt. From these incorrect evaluations, wrong tactics cannot help but develop.

The Communist Labor Party takes as its starting point the position that was taken by Lenin and the Communist International during the 1920's. That position is that the Negro question is not a race question or a question of a national minority, but a national question and an integral part of the world colonial revolution. Basing ourselves on the teachings of Marx, Engels, Lenin, Stalin and Mao Tsetung, "we must inevitably reach the conclusion that the self-determination of nations means the political separation of these nations from alien national bodies, and the formation of an independent national state."(3)

Since there is confusion concerning what is meant by a nation, we will give the definition developed by Stalin:

> A nation is a historically constituted, stable community of people, formed on the basis of a common language, territory, economic life, and psychological make-up manifested in a common culture.(4)

In bourgeois writing, the terms "race," "state" and "nation" are used interchangeably. "Race" is a term used primarily to describe physical characteristics such as skin color, hair texture and size of eyes, lips and nose. This term is very unscientific and has been used by many bourgeois governments to suit their own purposes: e.g., Nazi Germany classified their Japanese allies as members of the "Aryan Race." The USNA classified all Mexicans and Puerto Ricans as Caucasians. In South Africa, Japanese are classified as "honorary whites" while Chinese are classified as "colored." While nations belong in the category of history, a state belongs in the category of politics. A state is a political apparatus which one class uses to oppress another class—thus we have slave states, feudal states, capitalist states and socialist states. A state is not necessarily a national state. States are also multinational: the USNA, the USSR and the People's Republic of China are all multinational states.

An Historically Evolved People

The Negro people are historically as well as ethnically distinct from their African, Anglo-European or Indian ancestors. They were formed from diverse backgrounds as can be seen in the various groupings here and in Africa. From the different peoples which were at different stages of economic development and had different languages, gods and cultural backgrounds emerged a people with a common Negro nationality forged by centuries of chattel slavery in North America. The lash and the slave pen, the auction block and the breeding farm were the melting pot from which emerged the Negro people.

When the African slaves were brought to this country, they were broken in spirit. One tribal grouping was preferred for the cotton fields, another for the cane fields, another for artisan work. Both tribal temperament and stature were involved.

This process of being "broken in" was the common experience for all the African people that came to the American colonies. The Negro people are a mixture of these tribal groupings with the Indian

BY

HEWLETT & BRIGHT.

SALE OF

VALUABLE

SLAVES,

(On account of departure)

The Owner of the following named and valuable Slaves, being on the eve of departure for Europe, will cause the same to be offered for sale, at the NEW EXCHANGE, corner of St. Louis and Chartres streets, on *Saturday*, May 16, at Twelve o'Clock, *viz.*

1. SARAH, a mulatress, aged 45 years, a good cook and accustomed to house work in general, is an excellent and faithful nurse for sick persons, and in every respect a first rate character.

2. DENNIS, her son, a mulatto, aged 24 years, a first rate cook and steward for a vessel, having been in that capacity for many years on board one of the Mobile packets; is strictly honest, temperate, and a first rate subject.

3. CHOLE, a mulatress, aged 36 years, she is, without exception, one of the most competent servants in the country, a first rate washer and ironer, does up lace, a good cook, and for a barbelow who wishes a housekeeper she would be invaluable; she is also a good ladies' maid, having travelled to the North in that capacity.

4. FANNY, her daughter, a mulatress, aged 16 years, speaks French and English, is a superior hair-dresser, (pupil of Guillac,) a good seamstress and ladies' maid, is smart, intelligent, and a first rate character.

5. DANDRIDGE, a mulatto, aged 26 years, a first rate dining-room servant, a good painter and rough carpenter, and has but few equals for honesty and subjects.

6. NANCY, his wife, aged about 24 years, a confidential house servant, good seamstress, mantuamaker and tailoress, a good cook, washer and ironer, etc.

7. MARY ANN, her child, a creole, aged 7 years, speaks French and English, is smart, active and intelligent.

8. FANNY or FRANCES, a mulatress, aged 22 years, is a first rate washer and ironer, good cook and house servant, and has an excellent character.

9. EMMA, an orphan, aged 10 or 11 years, speaks French and English, has been in the country 7 years, has been accustomed to waiting on table, sewing etc., is intelligent and active.

10. FRANK, a mulatto, aged about 32 years speaks French and English, is a first rate hostler and coachman, understands perfectly well the management of horses, and is, in every respect, a first rate character, with the exception that he will occasionally drink, though not as habitual drunkard.

All the above named slaves are acclimated and excellent subjects; they were purchased by their present vendor many years ago, and will, therefore, be severally warranted against all vices and maladies prescribed by law, save and except FRANK, who is fully guaranteed in every other respect but the one above mentioned.

TERMS:—One-half Cash, and the other half in notes at six months, drawn and endorsed to the satisfaction of the Vendor, with special mortgage on the Slaves until final payment. The Acts of Sale to be passed before WILLIAM BOSWELL, Notary Public, at the expense of the Purchaser.

New-Orleans, May 13, 1835.

Source: Langston Hughes & Milton Meltzer, A Pictorial History of the Negro in America (New York: Crown Publishers, Inc., 1956)

and Anglo-European strain very noticeable. The latter strain is due primarily to the wholesale rape of Negro women.

Around the edges of slavery was the poor Anglo-American minority who wrung a living from the poorer soil overlooked by the planter. They worked as sharecroppers, as guards, or sometimes as whip hands. Generally their life was a little better than the slaves. Their destinies then as now were conditioned by the struggle and conditions of the Negro masses.

A Stable Community of People

The migration of Negro people during the 1920's and post World War II years to the Anglo-American Nation is a point always raised by "clever Marxists" to show the disappearing of the Negro Nation. These "clever Marxists" deal with percentages and not absolute numbers. From 1860 to 1960 the percentage of Negroes to Anglo-Americans in the South as a region declined from 36% to 20%. In fact, in the period from 1940 to 1963 the South lost 3,300,000 Negroes. These figures serve as the basis for all the claims the revisionists make concerning the stability of the Negro people. Well, let us look at some other figures.

More than five million Irish have immigrated to the USNA, most of them coming during the period of the Potato Famine in Ireland. Just because only four million remain, does this spell the end of the Irish nation? Of course not! Only a fool would reason otherwise. In the entire South (that region south of the Mason-Dixon line) the Negro population has shown a relative decline in percentage in relation to Anglo-American, but there has been a stable and absolute year-by-year growth of the Negro population. In 1860, there were roughly four million Negroes in the South; in 1910 about nine million and in 1960 eleven million. Today, 52% of all Negro people live in the South, roughly 15 million.

In the Negro Nation, or that area which includes the Black Belt and economically connected areas, there remain more than five million Negroes; and the out-migration from this area has ceased. In fact, since 1966 the Bureau of the Census has noted (in a special study) a definite trend toward immigration into the Negro Nation.

NEGRO POPULATION IN THE SOUTH

STATE	Total Negro Population				Negro %	
	1860	1910	1960	1970	1860	1970
Delaware	21,627	31,181	60,688	78,276	19.3	13.1
Maryland	171,131	232,250	518,410	701,341	24.9	17.1
D.C.	14,316	94,446	411,737	537,712	19.1	71.1
Virginia	548,907	671,098	816,258	865,388	34.4	18.6
W. Virginia	---------	74,173	89,317	73,931	-----	4.2
No. Carolina	361,522	697,843	1,116,021	1,137,644	36.4	20.5
So. Carolina	412,320	835,834	827,291	789,041	58.6	30.4
Georgia	465,698	1,176,987	1,122,569	1,190,779	44.1	25.8
Florida	62,677	308,669	880,136	1,049,578	44.6	15.4
Kentucky	236,167	261,656	215,949	241,292	20.0	7.4
Tennessee	283,019	473,088	588,876	631,696	25.5	16.0
Alabama	437,770	908,282	980,271	908,247	45.4	26.6
Mississippi	437,404	1,009,487	915,713	815,770	55.3	36.7
Arkansas	171,259	442,891	388,787	357,225	25.6	18.5
Louisiana	350,373	813,824	1,039,207	1,088,734	49.5	29.8
Oklahoma		137,612	153,984	177,907	-----	6.9
Texas	182,921	690,049	1,187,125	1,410,677	30.3	12.6
The SOUTH	4,079,000	8,749,000	11,311,607	12,064,258	36.8	19.2

Source: The American Negro Reference Book, John P. Davis, Ed.

A Stable Community of Language

The Negro people have a community of language which is English, the language of their oppressor nation. Every nation has its language, but different nations don't have to speak different languages. Brazil is a nation which speaks Portuguese, the language of its former oppressor. Mexico is a nation which speaks Spanish, the language of its former oppressor.

A stable community of language is necessary because otherwise it would be impossible to carry out a common economic life. Everyone in the Negro Nation communicates and carries out social and economic intercourse with a common language.

NEGRO POPULATION AS PERCENT OF TOTAL POPULATION
By County, 1970

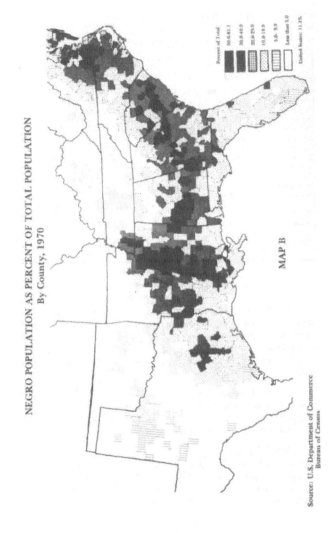

NEGRO POPULATION AS PERCENT OF TOTAL POPULATION
By County, 1970

Percent of Total

50.0–81.1

30.0–49.9

20.0–29.9

10.0–19.9

5.0–9.9

Less than 5.0

United States: 11.1%

MAP B

Source: U.S. Department of Commerce
Bureau of Census

64

MAP C

Geographic Distribution of Slave Population, 1790, 1800, 1830, and 1860

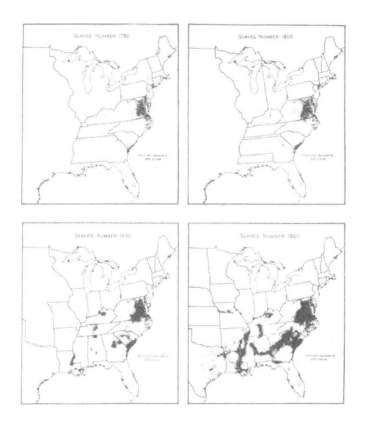

Source: E. Franklin Frazier, The Negro in the United States (New York: The Macmillan Company, 1957), Maps II, III, IV, and V.

MAP D

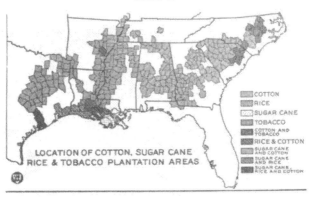

LOCATION OF COTTON, SUGAR CANE
RICE & TOBACCO PLANTATION AREAS

COTTON
RICE
SUGAR CANE
TOBACCO
COTTON AND TOBACCO
RICE & COTTON
SUGAR CANE AND COTTON
SUGAR CANE AND RICE
SUGAR CANE, RICE AND COTTON

Based on plantation census of 1910, supplemented by data obtained in special field investigations, 1920-21, in the newer developed sections. (From United States Department of Agriculture *Bulletin No.* 1269 "Relation of Land Tenure to Plantation Organization, by C. O. Brannen.

MAP E

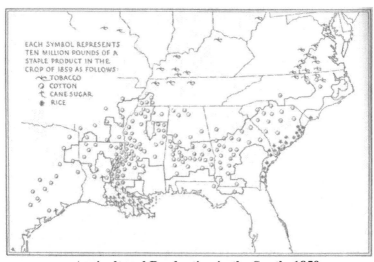

EACH SYMBOL REPRESENTS
TEN MILLION POUNDS OF A
STAPLE PRODUCT IN THE
CROP OF 1859 AS FOLLOWS:
— TOBACCO
◯ COTTON
↑ CANE SUGAR
❋ RICE

Agricultural Production in the South, 1859
Source: James S. Allen, The Negro Question in the United States
(New York: International Publishers, 1936)

MAP F

Cotton Production in 1930.
The outline of the 1930 Black Belt is also shown.
Source: James S. Allen, The Negro Question in the United States
(New York: International Publishers, 1936)

The 1972 census reported that 52% of all Negroes lived in the South. What the census doesn't report is that Negroes live in very specific areas of the South. This area of Negro concentration is within the "Black Belt." (See Map B) "Black Belt" refers to the rich and fertile black soil that stretches 1,600 miles long and 300 miles deep.

From Map C, showing the distribution of the slaves from 1790 to 1860, it can be seen that the slaves were concentrated in particular areas due to the crop that was being cultivated. Map D shows the crop distribution and Map E illustrates the location of the various large-scale plantations.

In 1664, Virginia and Maryland were producing twenty-five million pounds of tobacco annually, and by 1770 Virginia was exporting 100,000,000 pounds per year.

Rice was brought in from Madagascar in 1694 and before long it was being cultivated widely in the low-lying lands of the "Rice-coast" of the Carolinas, Georgia and upper Florida.

Indigo was introduced from the West Indies in 1743 and soon became a paying crop.

Sugar was cultivated in Louisiana as early as 1651, but it was not until 1797 when the problem of crystallizing the cane juice into sugar was solved that the crop began to take on commercial importance.

Cotton was planted in Jamestown as early as 1621, but owing to the difficulty of cleansing out the seeds, it remained for more than a century merely a garden plant. It was not until after the invention of the cotton gin in 1793 that cotton began its spectacular development and in its turn became "king" of the plantation economy. It can be seen from the maps that the distribution of crops corresponded with the territory inhabited by the Negro slaves.

Maps E and F show the concentration of cotton and other crops in 1930 and the concentration of Negroes. Quite a coincidence! Bui the revisionists and chauvinists say that the stable population and territory of Negroes has disappeared due to massive migration north. Map B shows the concentration of Negro people in the South in 1970. The breakdown by county shows unmistakably the stability of Negroes in areas based primarily around the old plantations.

In the strictest sense, the limits of the Negro Nation are the limits of the Black Belt and the surrounding area. But it is senseless to discuss national boundaries without discussing the peripheral areas that are economically dependent on them. Therefore, the historically evolved territory of the Negro Nation is the Black Belt plus the surrounding area that makes possible the economic and geographic entity we call the Nation.

Lenin points out:

> But the national composition of the population is one of the most important economic factors, not the only one, and not the most important. Towns, for example, play a most important economic role under capitalism, and elsewhere—in Poland, Lithuania, in the Ukraine, in Great Russia and elsewhere — it is the towns that are mostly distinguished for their mixed populations. To separate the towns from the villages and areas which economically gravitate towards them for the sake of the 'national' factor would be absurd and impossible. Marxists, therefore, must not take their stand entirely and exclusively on the national territorial principle.
>
> The solution to the problem indicated by the last con-

ference advanced the following thesis: 'There is a need for... extensive regional autonomy' (not for Poland alone, of course, but for all the regions of Russia) 'and completely democratic local self-governing and autonomous regions to be defined (the borders of the present gubernias, uzezds, etc.) but on the basis of the local inhabitants' assessment of the economic and social conditions and national composition of the population etc...'

Here the national composition of the population is put side by side with the other conditions (primarily economic, then social, etc.) which must serve as the basis for defining the new borders that will be suitable for modern capitalism and not for bureaucracy and Asiatic barbarism. All these conditions can be fully 'assessed' only by the local population, and on the basis of this assessment the central parliament of the state will define the borders of the autonomous regions and the limits of the jurisdiction of autonomous diets.(5)

Economic Community

Exchange between town and country indicates a common economic life. This economic life began developing before the Civil War and was based on producing and exporting agricultural products. During this period capitalism in the North was in a weak position due to the competition of the British for the South's market. The South supplied the raw material (cotton) for the textile mills of England while it got back finished products, cheaper than if it had bought them from the Northern Yankee bourgeoisie.

After the Civil War and the defeat of the Southern planters, Northern capital began to penetrate the South. This was especially evident after the birth of USNA imperialism and the crushing of Reconstruction in 1877. The major investment of Northern capital during this time was in railroads. Wall Street had taken over the Nashville Railroad during the economic crisis of 1873-1878. In 1893, J.P. Morgan created the Southern Railroad out of the remains of the Richmond and West Point Terminal Railroad. In 1907 Morgan took over Tennessee Coal and Iron and Railroad Company. Northern capital also invested heavily in lumber, coal, steel, tobacco and iron production. In the late 1880's the South was producing more iron than the whole nation was before the Civil War. The Negro Nation, which is less than 3% of the world's land, produced 55% of the world's cotton in 1928.

USNA imperialism began to mature about 1880, and by 1900 it was well developed. The political and economic life of the Negro Nation was subordinated to the needs of Anglo-American monopoly capital. The economic ties between town and country, along with the common banking, credit and monetary system which constituted an economic community, were reforged by the overwhelming power of Wall Street.

The social chauvinists (socialists in words, chauvinists in deeds) have delighted in pointing out that the Negro Nation (Black Belt and connected area) does not have a "separate economic system." Certainly, Brazil is controlled by USNA imperialism. The Brazilian economy is geared to and is part of the economy of the USNA. According to revisionist logic, imperialism by its nature destroys nations by destroying "separate economic structures." The continued existence of common economic exchange in nations like Brazil and the Negro Nation refute this chauvinist argument.

The indication of "common economic life" or "common economic community" is the existence of economic classes. The major classes in the Negro Nation are the comprador bourgeoisie, national bourgeoisie, peasantry (farmers) and the proletariat. However, in order to have a common economic life, or economic exchange, all that is necessary is the proletariat and the peasantry. That indicates exchange between town and country.

The comprador bourgeoisie is of historical necessity Negro. This is so because the market of the comprador is imperialism. The comprador of the Negro Nation has nothing to sell except the people. The Negro majority will not follow an Anglo-American traitor. That traitor has to be Negro in the same manner that the comprador of China had to be of the nationality of the majority of the Chinese. Mobuto's treachery could not be carried out by a Belgian national.

The comprador bourgeoisie is wholly an appendage of the international bourgeoisie, dependent upon imperialism for their survival and growth. Representatives of this class are found in the clergy, in political life, in the governmental bureaucracy and the upper stratum of the Negro college community.

The most important section of this comprador class is its Negro politicians. There were over 1,505 Negroes holding elective or appointive positions in state, municipal or county agencies in the South in 1975. These offices ranged from mayors, state senators, and sheriffs to library and community relations commissions. Charles Evers, Julian Bond, Walter Washington are a few of the nationally known Negro compradors, but there are also others more powerful, e.g., Leroy Johnson. According to Newsweek magazine, "Johnson, elected in 1962 as Georgia's first black state senator since Reconstruction, is probably the most powerful black politician in the South. He delivered the votes that elected Sam Massell as Atlanta's mayor; he even wields enough votes to intimidate Lester Maddox." Newsweek also reported on John L. McCown, a Negro businessman in Hancock County, Georgia, who used government funds and foundation grants to engineer a campaign to have himself "and his full slate of candidates for county commissions and school board swept into office."(6)

These comprador politicians are entirely dependent on the imperialist government of the USNA. As the struggle of the Negro people increases, this class will undoubtedly grow in order to maintain, for the USNA imperialists, control over the Negro Nation. In fact, there are already clear signs that the USNA imperialists are laying the groundwork for this type of solution of the Negro national colonial question. This is pointed out in the recent elections where more than 650 Negro legislators and officials were elected in the South. In Alabama, voters elected two Negro candidates to the state legislature, which has been all Anglo-American for nearly a century. In Greenwood County, Alabama, an entire slate of Negro legislators was elected. Alabama voters also elected four Negro sheriffs and a probate judge. A Baltimore college professor became the first Negro ever to be elected to Congress from Maryland. In another Maryland contest, a Negro was elected State's Attorney.

The Negro bourgeoisie, including the comprador section, has its historical roots among the freed slaves and house servants prior to the Civil War. The freed slaves had a virtual monopoly of the mechanical arts in the South. (For example, freed slaves made up 100,000 of the 125,000 artisans in the South at the end of the Civil War.) In 1860, the free "colored" people in New Orleans owned property valued at $15 million. In Charleston, South Carolina, 371 free persons of color including 13 Indians were paying taxes on real estate valued at about $1 million.

REGISTRATION RATES IN 11 SOUTHERN STATES, 1960-1970 (by percent)

State	1960	1964	1968	1970
Alabama	13.7	19.3	51.6	64
Arkansas	38.0	40.4	62.8	72
Florida	39.4	51.2	63.6	67
Georgia	29.3	27.4	52.6	64
Louisiana	31.1	31.6	58.9	62
Mississippi	5.2	6.7	59.8	68
N. Carolina	39.1	46.8	51.3	55
S. Carolina	13.7	37.3	51.2	57
Tennessee	59.1	69.5	71.7	77
Texas	35.5	N/A	61.6	85
Virginia	23.1	38.3	55.6	61

SOUTHERN BLACK ELECTED OFFICIALS, 1964-1974

State	1964	1965	1966	1967	1968	1974
Alabama	11	1	7	5	24	149
Arkansas					33	150
Florida		1	3	10	16	73
Georgia	2	10	6	3	21	137
Louisiana		3	7	27	37	149
Mississippi			1	28	29	191
N. Carolina		3		7	10	159
S. Carolina			7	4	11	116
Texas	1	4	7	3	15	124
Tennessee	1	6	16	3	26	87
Virginia	6	5	6	7	24	63

Source: Ronald Walters, The Black Politician, in Current History, Vol. 67, No. 399, November, 1974

Today, the Negro bourgeoisie is based primarily around 37 insurance companies, 40 savings and loan associations, and 20 banks exceeding half a billion dollars of total assets. The Negro capitalist class is also rooted in service industries (catering, maintenance), eating and drinking establishments, funeral homes, cosmetic manufacturing, gasoline stations, auto repair shops, barber and beauty shops, real estate dealers, brokers and owners of retail outlets. These businesses serve primarily a market overlooked or not considered profitable by big business—the segregated Negro areas and neighborhoods. Total assets of the "core" Negro financial institutions is a financially small but politically significant $1 billion.

There are a handful of millionaires, and there is a fairly large and growing number of prosperous families and individuals. In 1969, 1.6% of the Negroes in the South had incomes of $10,000 or more per year, while 93.4% of the Southern population as a whole had incomes under $10,000. That portion of this upper income stratum living in the Negro Nation does not feel the full effects of the oppression of the Negro masses. They have good homes, expensive cars, college educated children, yachts and country clubs.

The Negro national bourgeoisie traditionally has had a dual nature. On the one hand it has opposed monopoly capital because Wall Street has never allowed it to fully capture the vast Negro market—or even the more lucrative parts of it. On the other hand, the Negro national bourgeoisie has feared a confrontation with the power of Wall Street capital.

Especially since 1965, the open and quite successful tactic of the government has been to create the conditions where the Negro bourgeoisie relies on the government to assist in the securing of the market and the guaranteeing of profit through tax manipulation, government funding and assistance from the giant corporations in technical matters. The inevitable result of this "black capitalism" policy has been to almost eliminate the difference between the two wings of the Negro bourgeoisie. Consequently, both the comprador and the national bourgeoisie have eliminated themselves from the possibility of playing a leading role in the liberation struggles of the Negro people.

During the 1950's and early 1960's the leadership of the Negro national liberation movement was almost entirely in the hands of the Negro bourgeoisie. This can be seen from the demands that were made at that time. Desegregation and integration, to the extent that they took place, had a different meaning for the Negro bourgeoisie than for the Negro proletariat. For the Negro workers, the gains had to be limited to the position of the Anglo-American minority workers. But for the Negro capitalist, the sky was the limit. The Negro bourgeoisie could not fight alone, it had to have the muscle represented by the working class. Therefore, demands dear to the working class were raised, and in some cases gains were won by hard fighting and bloodshed. In such struggles, no matter what their color or nationality, the workers do the fighting and dying while the bourgeoisie reaps the profits. This was one of the reasons the struggle was acceptable to the imperialists and, in some instances, commenced and supported by them.

The Negro national working class includes the Anglo-American minority workers. Historical development places the proletariat of the Negro people as the vanguard of the working class in the Negro Nation. They have been raising and will continue to raise demands which are fundamentally in opposition to capitalist rule. The Negro proletariat has grown rapidly since 1947, as non-agricultural employment increased by 75% between 1946 and 1966 in the South as a region. This compares with a 38.2% increase for the continental USNA, and reflects the influx of profit-hungry industries since the end of W. W. II. Of the more than 7 million proletarians working in the manufacturing, contract, construction and transportation industries of the South, nearly 2½ million are concentrated in and around the Negro Nation. Over 50% of these proletarians are Negro and in 1960 more than 60% of all employed Negroes were employed in the South. The vanguard of the Negro working class is concentrated in the heavy industrial and transportation sectors of the economy, but recent years have also seen those workers employed in public services and farm labor take a leading role in the class struggle of the Negro Nation and the South as a region.

The leadership of the Negro people is shifting from the bourgeoisie to the proletariat. This has further radicalized the Negro people's struggle. In 1967, the Newport shipyard strike was led by Negro workers, but included a large number of Anglo-Americans. This strike developed such unity that the Chief of Police said that "the whites and blacks were fighting like brothers" against the police and scabs. The vanguard of the Negro working class also led the big hospital strikes in Atlanta, Georgia and Charleston, South Carolina, in 1969. From 1968 through 1970 militant strikes by sanitation workers throughout the South signaled the rising class consciousness of the Negro proletariat. During a 1968 strike, Martin Luther King, Jr., an exponent of non-violence and a tool of USNA imperialism, was forced to go South to channel the struggle of the striking sanitation workers onto a "safe" and "non-violent" road.

We can see from the mass uprisings across the Anglo-American Nation and in the Negro Nation that "non-violence" as a philosophy has been completely discredited and rejected by the Negro masses. It now remains for the CLP to unite and organize the Negro proletariat as the vanguard of the Negro national liberation struggle allied with the world's colonial masses and united with the Anglo-American proletariat. Only in this way can independence and Socialism be won.

Peasantry—Anchor of the Nation

No nation can exist without a peasantry to stabilize it in one locale. Stalin points this out in his criticisms of Bauer for his wrong view on a "Jewish" Nation:

...Among the Jews there is no large and stable stratum connected with the land, which would naturally rivet the nation together, serving not only as its framework but also as a national market.(7)

Agriculture was the basic purpose for the importation of African slaves into the American colonies. By 1850, some 2.8 million slaves lived within the confines of the cotton kingdom, working on farms and plantations. Of these, 1.8 million were engaged in cotton cultivation, with the remainder being used to raise tobacco, rice and sugar cane.

Emancipation and reconstruction did not radically alter the Negro's role in agriculture, particularly since he was not allowed to participate in the post-war homesteading movement. After 1865, Negro farm workers were the main source of cheap labor for cultivating the agricultural products of the South. In 1890, 25 years after the Civil War, 65% of all employed Negroes in the South were farmers or farm laborers. By 1920, Negro farm operators numbered 915,595 in the South. In 1965, about 9% of all Negro workers including women were principally in agriculture compared to 6% of all Anglo-American workers.

NUMBER, ACREAGE AND VALUE OF FARMS OPERATED BY NEGROES IN THE SOUTH: 1959, 1950 and 1920

Tenure of operator	Number of farms			Land in farms (Thousand acres)		
	1959	1950	1920	1959	1950	1920
Total	265,621	559,090	922,914	13,901	26,275	41,318
Full owners	89,749	141,482	178,558	5,577	8,391	11,950
Part owners	37,534	51,864	39,031	3,104	3,723	2,126
Managers	290	239	1,770	351	347	368
All tenants	138,048	365,505	703,555	4,869	13,815	26,874
Cash	14,855	39,562	100,275	784	2,097	4,011
Share cash	2,406	5,656	8,207	144	271	272
Crop share	31,714	95,461	176,711	1,410	4,424\	7,815
Livestock share	946	1,736'		73	136'	
Croppers	73,387	198,057	333,713	1,880	5,540	10,141
Others and unknown	14,740	25,033	84,649	576	1,346	4,636

	Average Acres per farm			Average value of farms ($)		
	1959	1950	1920	1959	1950	1920
	52.3	47.0	44.8	6,240	2,792	2,414
Full owners	62.1	59.3	66.9	6,255	3,062	2,561
Part owners	82.7	71.8	54.5	9,436	4,165	2,241
Managers	1211.0	1451.1	207.9	107,072	43,661	12,166
All tenants	35.3	37.8	38.2	5,284	2,464	2,352
Cash	52.8	53.0	40.0	4,299	2,021	2,016
Share cash	60.0	47.9	33.1	8,297	3,532	3,668
Crop share	44.5	46.3	44.2	6,880	2,906	2,765
Livestock share	77.1	78.5		11,587	4,908	
Croppers	25.6	28.0	30.4	4,809	2,311	2,190
Others and unknown	39.1	53.8	54.8	4,166	2,266	2,397

Source: 1959 Census of Agriculture, Volume II.

From the above chart, we can see the various stratifications among Negro farmers. An analysis of the conditions and attitudes of the various categories can be found in Mao Tsetung's Analysis of Classes in Chinese Society and Lenin's Capitalism in Agriculture.

Negro owners (full and part) numbered 127,000 and controlled 8.7 million acres of land in 1959. That is a little more than 13,000 square miles, an area the size of Connecticut, Massachusetts and Rhode Island combined. The vast majority of Negro farmers in the USNA today are in the tobacco and cotton country of eastern North and South Carolina and the cotton belt lying 50 miles north and 75 miles south of Memphis, Tennessee.

Cotton, tobacco, and "other field crops" amount to 92% of all Southern Negro farms operated at the commercial level. "Other field crops" consist principally of peanut and soy bean specialty farms in North Carolina and Georgia. In the fall of 1959, 56% of the commercial size farms run by Negroes were cotton farms. In Arkansas, 94% of all commercial farmers were cotton specialists in 1959.

There has been a trend, developed during and after World War I, that prolonged the role of Negroes in agriculture. This was the rise of cigarette smoking. Much of the tobacco used was grown only in the South, predominantly in sections where many Negro farmers were already present. The average Negro-owned farm was well suited to tobacco, which was grown strictly by hand and animal labor. Tobacco growing did not require much land. Between 1910 and 1945, the number of Negro tobacco growers rose from 42,000 to 91,000. Negro operated farms growing tobacco account for 18% of all cigarette tobacco grown, whereas 10% of all cotton was grown by Negro operated cotton farms (1959). Of the principal cigarette-type (flue-cured) tobacco, Negro farmers accounted for 25% of the crop.

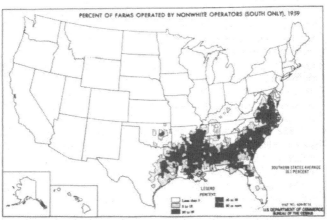

Source: John P. Davis, The American Negro Reference Book
(Englewood Cliffs, New Jersey: Prentice-Hall, Inc., 1969)

There has been a steady over-all decline in the numbers of the Negro peasantry. This "fleeing the land" process is the main point that the revisionist CPUSA and other "leftist" groups seize upon to "prove" the disappearance of the Negro Nation. There is an old saying that "figures don't lie, but liars can figure." This is exactly what the Anglo-American chauvinists do in describing the process of Negroes leaving the farms for the urban areas. When Marxists analyze any social process, they always study it in its inter-relationship with other processes.

The first massive migration of Negroes out of the "South" appears to have started about 1915 and to have continued at a high rate during most of the next ten years. Several factors were responsible for this migration. One reason was the boll weevil, a beetle which lays its eggs in cotton balls and whose larvae consume the cotton, had entered southern Texas from Mexico in the 1890's. By 1921, it had spread over the entire Cotton Belt. The boll weevil caused great panic as millions of acres of cotton were heavily damaged and production fell. The sections most susceptible to damage were those with heavy slow-warming soils, such as in the Black Belt of Alabama, where the majority of farmers were Negroes. In these sections, cotton never regained its prominence, and thousands of Negroes emigrated as the landlords returned to livestock and dairying. In the rolling Piedmont country of Georgia and South Carolina, severe erosion and soil depletion added to the problem and impelled other thousands to leave or look for industrial work.

PERCENTAGE OF COTTON HARVEST
BY MACHINE AND BY HAND

AREA	1950	1957	1962
SOUTH (Except Texas & Oklahoma)			
Machine	1%	11%	55%
Hand	99%	89%	45%
TEXAS & OKLAHOMA			
Machine	11%	38%	78%
Hand	89%	62%	22%

This chart also indicates the growth of the big industrial farm and the dying away of the small family type farm in the South.

In the years just prior to World War II, the future character of cotton farming in the USNA became noticeable. In the northern part of the Mississippi Delta country, hundreds of tenant people were "tractored off" the cotton plantations. Mules were replaced by tractors and vast numbers of families were displaced. In the same period, the mechanical cotton picker was being developed and it was obviously only a matter of time before it would be perfected.

The major factor inducing migration from the South was the First World War. Immigration of Europeans to the USNA, which had been bringing more than a million persons a year to Northern industrial cities, was cut off. The war, even before direct USNA "involvement," brought new demands upon Northern manufacturing industries. Industries which had been providing hundreds of thousands of jobs each year for new immigrants now had this cheap labor supply cut off during a period of great demand for labor. Many firms not only discovered the Negro proletariat, but sent out labor recruiters to the South to encourage Negroes to come north. Many Negroes who made the move encouraged friends and relatives to join them. Other factors responsible for driving Negro farmers off the land and into the cities were the increased use of synthetic material and the cheaper cotton imported from Egypt and Pakistan. In addition, cutbacks in tobacco production have been responsible for forcing many Negroes out of commercial farming.

We can see from these factors that the Negro peasantry has been on the decline. But this phenomenon isn't limited to Negroes alone.

Migration of Anglo-Americans from Southern farms during the decade of the 1960's is estimated at 43%, even though the rate for Negroes was 63%. From the various charts, we see the number of Negro farmers diminishing whereas the number of Negro farm laborers has been growing. A Negro rural proletariat has been created. In April, 1950, the South's 392,000 Anglo-American hired farm workers had declined to 308,000 while hired Negro farm workers had increased to 311,000. For the first time Negroes made up over half of the South's farm wage workers. In the South, where Negro farmers comprise only one-sixth of all farmers, Negro workers make up fully one-half of all farm wage workers.

From these facts it can be seen that even though the number of Negro farmers has declined, the number of rural proletarians has increased. There remains today a stable, though small, population of

Negroes based primarily around farming. In addition, it should be mentioned that there are within the Black Belt area approximately one million "landless peasants" who remain on the land but who are not for the most part included in commercial agricultural statistics. These people survive off welfare, part-time jobs and small gardens.

Joseph Stalin pointed out that "...after all, the peasant question is the basis, the quintessence of the national question."(8) In other words, the question of territory and land redistribution is a key aspect of the national question. The size of the peasantry is not the primary factor. As long as a peasantry exists, a nation will remain anchored to a given territory. This fact in turn means that the national question can only be settled by the liberation and redistribution of the lands worked by the oppressed farmers, wage laborers and landless peasants who are the "anchor of the nation." Certainly, no progressive person would deny that the independence of Puerto Rico can only come about through some form of land redistribution, and the ratio of peasants to workers in that country is only one to twenty-six.

As shown above, a relatively large peasantry, or "anchor," holds the Negro Nation to a general area embracing thousands of square miles of territory. Like the Puerto Rican national colonial question, the Negro national colonial question can only be solved by a return of the land to the people who have toiled over it for centuries. In the Negro Nation this land redistribution will demand a combination of state farms and cooperative enterprises in order to best meet the needs of the people under the conditions of modern mechanized agriculture.

It should be added that in this era of moribund capitalism, national liberation and the redistribution of land can only be accomplished by a united front of workers and peasants under the leadership of a Marxist-Leninist party.

Community of Culture

Stalin points out that apart from the community of language, territory, and economic life,

> one must take into consideration the specific spiritual complexion of the people constituting a nation. Nations differ not only in their conditions of life, but also in spiritual complexion, which manifests itself in peculiarities of national culture.

Negro people have a distinct national character due to their common history of slavery, segregation and national oppression. This common background of slavery merged the slaves into a distinct people before the rise of the Negro Nation. The slavery, segregation and discrimination based on color created the conditions for a common culture. This historical factor, the basis for the community of culture, shows us that the Anglo-American minority of the Negro Nation—although an integral part of that Nation—cannot be other than a minority of the Negro Nation because the root and base of the Negro Nation was the ex-slaves in the plantation areas.

The motivating force which has produced this common culture is the historical fact of slavery. From the days of the plantation, the Negro people were bound together in a special way by the common experience of chattel slavery. This exploitation and oppression excluded them from the culture of the Anglo-American Nation and forced them to create their own culture. The original diversity of tribal cultures, which their forefathers brought over with them from Africa was mostly stamped out under the fierce pressures of slavery, although some traces still persist. Many Negro women still wrap their heads in styles that are definitely African in origin. This custom developed in order to keep the hair clean from the dirt in the field and the lice and ticks of the slave quarters. Today, this custom still continues even though modern silk scarves are used.

The development of music, literature, poetry and all of the aspects of a national character which become manifested in a distinctive culture bear the imprint of the oppression of the Negro people and their struggle against the slavers' whip. To take a specific example, the present day "soul music" of the Negro people can be traced back to slave times. The soul of the African slave spoke to all men through the "sorrow songs." W. E. B. DuBois writes that the Negro folksong is the sole North American music—"it still remains as the singular spiritual heritage of the nation and the greatest gift of the Negro people." (1 0) Through these songs of their oppression and dreams of a better life came the articulate message of the slave to the world. These songs were transmitted primarily through the vehicle of the Negro church. DuBois states:

> The music of Negro religion is that plaintive rhythmic melody with its touching minor cadences, which, despite caricature and defilement, still remains the most original

and beautiful expression of human life and longing yet born on American soil. Sprung from African forests, where its counter-part can still be heard, it was adapted, changed and intensified by the tragic soul life of the slaves, until, under the stress of law and whip it became the one true expression of a people's sorrow, despair and hope. (11)

This music was unique to the Negro Nation because it was produced under the particularly brutal experience of slavery and the post-reconstruction national oppression under fascism.

Music is one aspect of Negro culture that has influenced and penetrated Anglo-American culture as no other has. Africa's contribution to music was the invention of the violin, xylophone, harp, flute, zither, guitar and some sources say also the tambourine. When African slaves arrived in the new world they improvised a new music based around the slave work songs and spirituals which voiced their sufferings and aspirations. The banjo, which was invented by a slave, was the basic instrument for the riverboat songs. Many of the songs on the waterfront were originated by the Negro stevedores, although Stephen Foster received credit for many by publishing them in his name. The evolution of Negro music has passed from "spirituals" to blues, popular (rhythm and blues) and to modern jazz with each category having its own variations.

Negro migrations north had great influence on the music in the Anglo-American Nation, and told of the different type of hardships Negroes met in the large urban centers. Negro music in the Anglo-American Nation has gone through a transformation from a merging of Negro and Anglo-American musical idioms. This has produced artists like the Chambers Brothers, Jimi Hendrix, Sly and the Family Stone and the Fifth Dimension with both Negro national minority and Anglo-Americans as their audiences. Many Anglo-American musicians have become famous by trying to imitate Negro musicians and entertainers: Al Jolson, Stephen Foster, Elvis Presley, and Tom Jones, for example. The Beatles were honest in saying that Negro music was the inspiration for many of their songs. They proved this by going to Tennessee to study Negro musical techniques.

Negro literature and folk tales have a rich background in the experiences of the slaves. Animal stories which were very popular in Africa went through a transformation in the new world due to the different animals and environment. In the African prototypes of the Negro tales the heroes were generally the jackal, the hare, the tortoise and the spider. The African jackal survived as the North American fox, the African hare as the North American rabbit, and the African tortoise as the North American dry-land turtle. As a villain the African hyena was replaced by the North America wolf, but that role is sometimes assigned to the fox or the bear.

These animal tales and folk stories are remembered in Uncle Remus and Brer Rabbit stories told by Joel Chandler Harris. Other Negro literature includes stories on slavery (including "swapping dreams"), preacher and the devil stories, ghost stories, sermons, ballads (e.g. John Henry), street cries and blues.

Negro customs such as national cuisine (soul food) and religious life are very distinct from that in the Anglo-American Nation. It can be seen today that the custom of eating pigs' feet, neck bones, black-eyed peas, greens, yams, and chitterlings are all associated with the region of the South, particularly the Negro Nation.

"Soul," this elusive substance, is nothing more than the national characteristic of the Negro people. The dynamics of Negro culture have always been an integral part of the continuous struggle to gain the posture of a free people.

In conclusion, it should be pointed out that a nation, like every other historical phenomenon, is subject to the law of change, has its history, its beginning and its end. It should also be remembered that none of the above-discussed characteristics of Negro nationhood is by itself sufficient to prove the existence of a nation. On the other hand, as Stalin pointed out, it is sufficient for a single one of the characteristics to be absent and the nation would cease to be a nation.

CHAPTER FIVE

MARXISM AND THE NATIONAL COLONIAL QUESTION

Joseph Stalin remains today the leading Marxist-Leninist theoretician on the national colonial question. We offer in this short section a summary of the position of Marxism-Leninism on this question.

The *third point* is the disclosure of the organic connection between the national and colonial question and the question of the rule of capital, of overthrowing capitalism, of the dictatorship of the proletariat. In the epoch of the Second International, the national question, narrowed down to the extreme, was usually regarded as an isolated question, unrelated to the coming proletarian revolution. It was tacitly assumed that the national question would be settled "naturally," before the proletarian revolution, by means of a series of reforms within the framework of capitalism; that the proletarian revolution could be accomplished without a radical settlement of the national question, and that, on the contrary, the national question could be settled without overthrowing the rule of capital, without, and before, the victory of the proletarian revolution. That essentially imperialist view runs like a red thread through the well-known works of Springer and Bauer on the national question. But the past decade has exposed the utter falsity and rottenness of this conception of the national question. The imperialist war has shown, and the revolutionary experience of recent years has again confirmed that:

1) the national and colonial questions are inseparable from the question of emancipation from the rule of capital;

2) imperialism (the highest form of capitalism) cannot exist without the political and economic enslavement of the unequal nations and colonies;

3) the unequal nations and colonies cannot be liberated without overthrowing the rule of capital;

4) the victory of the proletariat cannot be lasting without the liberation of the unequal nations and colonies from the yoke of imperialism.

If Europe and America may be called the front or the

arena of the major battles between socialism and imperialism, the unequal nations and colonies, with their raw materials, fuel, food and vast store of man-power, must be regarded as the rear, the reserve of imperialism. To win a war it is necessary not only to triumph at the front, but also to revolutionise the enemy's rear, his reserves. Hence, the victory of the world proletarian revolution may be regarded as assured only if the proletariat is able to combine its own revolutionary struggle with the liberation movement of the labouring masses of the unequal nations and the colonies against the rule of the imperialists and for the dictatorship of the proletariat. This "trifle" was overlooked by the leaders of the Second and Two-and-a-Half Internationals, who divorced the national and colonial question from the question of power in the epoch of growing proletarian revolution in the West.(1)

Stalin further spelled out the relationship between proletarian revolution and the national and colonial question in his *Foundations of Leninism:*
... In solving the national question Leninism proceeds from the following theses:

a) the world is divided into two camps: the camp of a handful of civilized nations, which possess finance capital and exploit the vast majority of the population of the globe; and the camp of the oppressed and exploited peoples in the colonies and dependent countries, which constitute that majority;

b) the colonies and the dependent countries, oppressed and exploited by finance capital, constitute a vast reserve and a very important source of strength for imperialism;

c) the revolutionary struggle of the oppressed peoples in the dependent and colonial countries against imperialism is the only road that leads to their emancipation from oppression and exploitation;

d) the most important colonial and dependent countries have already taken the path of the national liberation movement, which cannot but lead to the crisis of world capitalism;

e) the interests of the proletarian movement in the developed countries and of the national liberation movement in the colonies call for the union of these two forms of the revolutionary movement into a common front against the common enemy, against imperialism;

f) the victory of the working class in the developed countries and the liberation of the oppressed peoples from the yoke of imperialism are impossible without the formation and the consolidation of a common revolutionary front;

g) the formation of a common revolutionary front is impossible unless the proletariat of the oppressor nations renders direct and determined support to the liberation movement of the oppressed peoples against the imperialism of its "own country," for "no nation can be free if it oppresses other nations" (*Engels*);

h) this support implies the upholding, defence and implementation of the slogan of the right of nations to secession, to independent existence as states;

i) unless this slogan is implemented, the union and collaboration of nations within a single world economic system, which is the material basis for the victory of world socialism, cannot be brought about;

j) this union can only be voluntary, arising on the basis of mutual confidence and fraternal relations among peoples.(2)

EX-SLAVE WITH A LONG MEMORY, ALABAMA, 1937

Source: The Woman's Eye [Photo: Dorothy Lange],
(New York: Alfred A. Knopf, 1973)

CHAPTER SIX

THEORETICAL DEVIATIONS ON THE NEGRO NATIONAL COLONIAL QUESTION

Of the many current viewpoints on the national colonial question in the United States of North America, most deviate in one of two basic ways from a scientific analysis, i.e., from a Marxist-Leninist position. The general and primary type of deviation is national chauvinism; the other is reactionary cultural nationalism.

Chauvinism is linked to imperialism and as such maintains the domination of one nation over another. The specific role of white supremacy in the history of the USNA makes it inevitable that the most aggressive and brutal specific form of national chauvinism is white chauvinism. But, by no means be deceived that this national chauvinism is never directed toward Anglo-Europeans. Any European will tell you otherwise. This even rubs off on Negroes—so they sometimes tend to slander or discriminate against other peoples of other nations. We have all observed this idiotic situation. What we are trying to make clear is that the old white supremacy that justified slavery was supplanted by national chauvinism.

The new ideology of aggressive imperialism of the USNA had to assume certain forms of its forerunner—white supremacy. But it would be politically dangerous for us not to see the difference. White chauvinism is the leading and specific form of Anglo-American national chauvinism. White chauvinism provides the excuse for the brutal exploitation of the colored nations and peoples of the world—white chauvinism is a form that the social bribery takes to the Anglo-American people that prevents the unity of the working class and has hampered the building of a party of the class. White chauvinism is the principal ideology of aggressive USNA fascism. In the USNA we always find the other principal fascist ideology, anti-communism, tightly linked to and generally expressed as white chauvinism. So we see that here in the USNA the major ideological battle to be fought is against this fascist ideology.

Chauvinism is a concept that does away with class outlooks and substitutes for such outlooks the national imperialist outlook. Communism emphasizes the class struggle and class outlooks. The opposition to chauvinism of any type is the clarion call of the Third International, "Workers and Oppressed Peoples of the World,

Unite." What, then is the connection between these hostile, antagonistic ideas? The connection between these antagonisms is imperialism itself. Imperialism, while relying on chauvinism, cannot help but create the conditions and the motives to make "Workers of the World, Unite" a living reality. This is true because imperialism creates the material conditions for the unity of the class. Imperialism calls into existence a proletariat wherever it goes. It develops the necessary means of communication. Even though imperialism has to resort to the tactics of bribery in attempting to achieve national unity against the colonial workers, it cannot succeed. In the final analysis, imperialism unites first the colonial workers and, when it is compelled to attack the majority of the workers in the imperialist nations, the political conditions for the unity of all the workers and oppressed peoples of the world will mature.

Speaking in terms of history, we see how, on the one hand, white supremacy grew with Anglo-American expansionism. So long as there was no real economic use for white supremacy in the English colonies, it did not develop. As a matter of fact, leading Indians were presented to the courts of England and France as well as the Netherlands and Spain. It was only with the need to clear the western parts of the original colonies that the concept of white supremacy arose.

> Those sober virtuosi of Protestantism, the Puritans of New England, in 1703, by decrees of their assembly set a premium of £40 on every Indian scalp and every captured redskin; in 1720 a premium of £100 on every scalp; in 1744, after Massachusetts Bay had proclaimed a certain tribe as rebels, the following prices: for a male scalp 12 years and upwards, £100 (new currency), for a male prisoner £105, women and children prisoners £50, for scalps of women and children, £50.(1)

This, in the context of an economy where £1 per week was considered a fairly good wage. Needless to say, in a relatively short time the colonies were cleared of Indians. The scum of the earth had enmassed fortunes that they invested in the new cheap lands and the saying, "The only good Indian is a dead Indian" became part of the Anglo-American language.

In the Northern colonies, slavery proved to be an unprofitable venture except in the case of house servants, and they could more easily be hired than purchased. One by one, the most northern states abolished slavery. Not true in the South. Little by little, indentured servitude was replaced by complete chattel slavery. Alongside of this growth was the excuse of bringing the Africans here to make Christians of them. When this no longer sufficed, the concept of a color superiority slowly emerged. At first it was expressed with laws separating Anglo-European slaves from African slaves; laws prohibiting miscegenation; finally, laws prohibiting any form of social equality developed. With the insatiable greed of the plantations for slaves, Negro became the word for slave as much as Slav was the word for slave in the Roman empire. The ideological rationale outran the realities. Even in the field of language, black and evil, black and crude, black and unpleasant, became the unconscious expression of a system gone mad. Blackguard, blackmail, blackluck and countless other expressions indicated the tidal wave of white supremacy that was generated by the most profitable system devised by man.

Would the rising capitalist class defend such an important category in the superstructure? It absolutely had to. It might be asked, "why did the North co-exist with and even assist the slaveowners?" The reason is that until the 1850's the main wealth of the North was gained by the sale of meats, cloth and other necessaries to the slave areas. So we see that the entire country was involved with and dependent on slavery and that was the reason why white supremacy found fertile soil in all parts of the country. Only with the development of the contradiction—when the productive capacity of the North outran the consuming capacity of the South—did the struggle for political power and the need for the exclusion of foreign and especially English commodities became areas of sharp economic and therefore social struggle. Only then was the question of the democratic rights of Negroes raised.

Therefore, it is clearly shown that the basis of the gigantic strength of USNA capitalism lies in the fact that the land was acquired by slaughter of the Indians; that the wealth was accumulated by the free labor of the slaves. Hence, the oppression and exploitation of Indians and African slaves became a matter of the utmost national economic importance. Would not such an important matter be reflected in the superstructure? Just compare the free-wheeling development of the USNA capitalist with his free land and nearly free labor, to the lot of the English or French capitalist who had to rent his land from the former nobility, which still held a strangle-hold on the bourgeoisie, and at the same time had to face a rebellious labor force. Small wonder that the most vulgar chauvinism had permeated every aspect of life in the USNA.

Post-Civil War history complicated the situation even further. USNA imperialism emerged as a modern imperialism—as exporter of finance capital—and never really went through the stage of mercantile imperialism in the same way as the French or British imperialists.

USNA imperialism not only emerged late, but starting off as an exporter of capital, it had different demands than had the French or British imperialists whose base in mercantile imperialism demanded that they secure direct colonies. The main thrust of USNA imperialism was not toward the acquisition of direct colonies, but against it. Hence, Lincoln assisted Juarez in kicking the French and Austrians out of Mexico. Teddy Roosevelt kicked the Spanish out of the Caribbean and the Philippines and out-flanked the Portuguese, French and Spanish in Latin America. The USNA imperialists struggled for and were ready to fight for the "open door" in China rather than its partition into direct colonies.

It was impossible for the USNA imperialists to attempt to expand into the "white areas" of the world. The backward areas of Europe (Ireland, the Balkans, Eastern Europe) were conquered or being conquered by the great powers. There was nothing left for colonization except the backward colored areas of the earth. At any rate, the enslavement of the colored Central and South America, the conquests in the Caribbean, the emergence of the Negro Nation, the conquest of the Philippines, all added on to the concepts of color superiority that were left over from the history of slavery. However, it is obvious that the modern imperialists were not interested in the capture and enslavement of one individual or grouping of individuals. No, modern imperialism enslaved whole nations. Hence, white supremacy turned into white chauvinism, in as much as the enslaved nations were colored and the ruling class of the USNA was white.

The Anglo-American "revolutionaries" in the USNA who are blinded by white chauvinism either ignore or down play the importance of the national question, particularly as it related to the Negro Nation. Some typical chauvinist errors are: "there is no national question in the USNA and the special oppression of the Negro people is the result of *racism* and class oppression" or, "there may be a Negro Nation in the USNA, but national independence is not the way to solve the question, because the Negro people have not yet raised the demand for independence." Another chauvinist position advanced in the USNA holds that "all national movements are reactionary and must be defeated." Finally, we see that the basis of revisionism on the national question is William Z. Foster's "National Exceptionalism," or the idea that the Negro Nation is a "nation within a nation" and therefore an exceptional instance in the history of colonial and oppressed nations and not in conformity with the basic Leninist laws on imperialism. In essence, this position held by Foster and others fails to deal with the national question as a question involving territory with discernible boundaries. This position seeks to obscure the reality of the Negro Nation oppressed by the USNA imperialist state. Consequently, the reactionary, multinational character of the USNA state is blurred.

Back in 1953, when the CPUSA was still making an attempt at fighting white chauvinism, Foster, Chairman of the CP, wrote, "White chauvinism, the poisonous ideology of white supremacy..."(2) That might sound like an innocent enough statement, but it will not bear examination. What is white supremacy? White supremacy evolved as the ideological rationale for slavery. Again we should note that it was a rationale based on color—something the CPUSA has transformed into a question of "race." To state that white chauvinism is the ideology of white supremacy is to say that white supremacy is a material force and that white chauvinism is its ideological expression. Within the Marxist circle, chauvinism is accepted as linked to national privilege, especially during the period of imperialism. The confusion lies in the fact that just as USNA imperialism had its roots in the chattel slave system, so white chauvinism had its roots in the ideology of white supremacy. As the enslavement of dark-skinned individuals grew into the enslavement of a nation, so white supremacy grew into white chauvinism.

Further, Foster states, "white chauvinism originally developed by the Southern planters as a defense of chattel slavery has been taken up by the capitalists generally as one of the most dangerous of all their ideological weapons against the working class and its democratic allies." Here again we see the ideological and political confusion that marked the writings of the CP leaders and especially Foster. White chauvinism could not have been developed by the Southern planters. It could only have been developed in the era of imperialism. According to Foster, modern French chauvinism could be equated with the white supremacy of the slave-owning class in the 1800's. Such ideological confusion will not stand the test of investigation. We cannot buy a concept that does not change with a changing material basis. Chauvinism is linked with the conquest and enslavement of nations, not *races*. One of the reasons that the CP could not win the fight against chauvinism and chauvinists within the Party is that they never had a really clear understanding of chauvinism and the historical and political role that it has played.

Incorrect theory leads without fail to incorrect political programs and slogans. This is certainly true of the chauvinist ideas and theories which have been projected into political programs and slogans. For instance, take the common slogan which says "fight racism." This slogan implies that the solution lies in Anglo-Americans defeating their own *racist* ideas by repudiating self. As previously mentioned, this approach reduces the national liberation struggle to a battle of ideas and forces a division between Negro and Anglo-American workers.

The "left" advocates of white chauvinism in the USNA all attempt to pass themselves off as Marxist-Leninists by hiding beneath such Marxist slogans as "workers of the world unite" and "combat reactionary nationalism." But what is the specific position of Marxism-Leninism toward white chauvinism? The position expressed by Lenin, Stalin and Mao Tsetung on great-power chauvinism (which is concretely expressed in the USNA as white chauvinism) is that it is the ideological justification for imperialist oppression. Lenin pointed out in supporting Plekhanov's 1902 defense of the "right of nations to self-determination" that:

> this demand, while not obligatory upon bourgeois democrats was 'obligatory on Social Democrats.' If we were to forget it or hesitate to advance it... for fear of offending the national prejudices of our fellow countrymen of Great Russian nationality, the call... workers of all countries unite, would be a shameful lie on our lips...(3)

> Our model will always be Marx, who after living in Britain for decades and becoming half English, demanded freedom and national independence for Ireland in the interests of the socialist movement of the British workers.(4)

But the bourgeois radicals and mystifiers cry, "doesn't the bourgeois separatist movement gain support from the slogan Independence for the Negro Nation?" Concerning this, Lenin stated:

> We have seen that the following argument is one of R. Luxemburg's "trump cards" in her struggle against the programme of the Marxists in Russia: recognition of the right to self-determination is tantamount to supporting the bourgeois nationalism of the oppressed nations...
>
> The first argument, as Kautsky irrefutably proved nearly twenty years ago is a case of blaming other people for one's own nationalism; in her fear of the nationalism of the bourgeoisie of oppressed nations, R. Luxemburg is actually playing into the hands of the Black Hundred nationalism of the Great Russians.(5)

Yet the petty bourgeoisie, fearing the revolution, hold up another traitor's hesitation. They say "doesn't this program of national independence split the proletariat?" Lenin also answered this question:

> ...is it not clear that the more liberty the Ukrainian nationality enjoys in any particular country, the stronger its ties with the country will be? One would think that this truism could not be disputed without totally abandoning all the premises of democracy. Can there be greater freedom of nationality, as such than the freedom to secede, the freedom to form an independent national state?(6)

And further:

> the reactionaries are opposed to freedom of divorce; they say that it must be handled carefully and loudly declare that it means the 'disintegration of the family.' The democrats, however, believe that the reactionaries are hypocrites and that they are actually defending the omnipotence of the police and the bureaucracy, the privileges of one of the sexes, and the worst kind of oppression of women. They believe that in actual fact freedom of divorce will not cause the "disintegration" of family ties, but, on the contrary, will strengthen them on a democratic basis, which is the only possible and durable basis in civilized society.
> To accuse those who support freedom of self-

determination, i.e., freedom to secede, of encouraging separatism, is as foolish and hypocritical as accusing those who advocate freedom of divorce of encouraging the destruction of family ties.(7)

And finally:

> The liberals' hostility to the principle of political self-determination of nations can have one and only one real class meaning, national-liberalism, defense of the state privilege of the Great Russian bourgeoisie.
>
> The interests of the working class and of its struggle against capitalism demand complete solidarity and the closest unity of the workers of all nations; they demand resistance to the nationalist policy of the bourgeoisie of every nationality. Hence, Social Democrats would be deviating from proletarian policy and subordinating the workers to the policy of the bourgeoisie if they were to repudiate the right of nations to self-determination, i.e., the right of oppressed nations to secede, or if they were to support all the national demands of the bourgeoisie of oppressed nations...
>
> In any case the hired workers will be an object of exploitation. Successful struggle against exploitation requires that the proletariat be free of nationalism, and be absolutely neutral so to speak, in the fight for supremacy that is going on among the bourgeoisie of the various nations. If the proletariat of any one nation gives the slightest support to the privileges of its own national bourgeoisie, that will inevitably arouse distrust among the proletariat of another nation: it will weaken the international class solidarity of the workers and divide them, to the delight of the bourgeoisie. Repudiation of the right of self-determination or to secession inevitably means, in practice, support for the privileges of the dominant nation.(8)

There is but one scientific and revolutionary demand around the Negro national colonial question. That is "Independence for the Negro Nation." Independence is necessary before a real self-determination can proceed. Self-determination means freedom to choose. This freedom to choose doesn't mean anything unless a nation is free to choose, i.e., independent. The proletariat of the Anglo- American and Negro Nations must resolutely oppose the bourgeois concepts of *racism* and *integration* as the cause and cure of the Negro people's oppression. The Communist Labor Party has always said that the struggle for integration is a struggle for the liberation and equality of the Negro people and the Negro national minority. We have supported the struggle for integration. But integration under capitalism is not possible. This is so because of the colonial enslavement of the Negro Nation. Colonial peoples carry with them their national oppression wherever they go. Second-class citizen is the highest classification that the colonial worker can achieve in social, economic and political life. Integration can't work because unequals cannot be integrated. Equality and freedom can only be achieved when all oppressed peoples are set free from imperialist bondage. The Communist Labor Party stands on the thesis of Marx that "labor cannot emancipate itself in the white skin where in the black it is branded"(9) and that "no nation can be free if it oppresses other nations."(10)

The Communist Labor Party speaks in the interests of the Anglo-American working class. Therefore, our demand of independence for the Negro Nation is not a demand from the Negro Nation, but an important part of the strategy of the Anglo-American proletariat in its struggle with the imperialists of the USNA.

The fact is that, as Dr. DuBois stated, the South politically controls the country and Wall Street controls the South. The people of New York or California did not vote for Senator Eastland of Mississippi, but his 22 years in the Senate have allowed him to head the decisive Judiciary Committee. Therefore, he effectively controls legislation for the whole of the country. This legislative control of the country through the South is a main weapon in bourgeois democracy. By way of example, it should be noted that in 1975 the following committees were headed by fascists from the states that in part make up the Negro Nation.

Senate

Agriculture and Forestry	Talmadge (Ga.) Ch.*
Appropriations	McClellan (Ark.) Ch.
Defense sub committee	McClellan (Ark.) Ch.
Intelligence sub-committee	McClellan (Ark.) Ch.
Armed Services	Stennis (Miss.) Ch.
Intelligence sub-committee	Stennis (Miss.)
Preparedness	Stennis (Miss.)
Banking—2nd ranking member	Sparkman (Ala.)
Housing sub-committee	Sparkman (Ala.) Ch.
District of Columbia	Eagleton (Mo.) Ch.
Finance	Russell Long (La.) Ch.
Foreign Relations	Sparkman (Ala.)
Judiciary	Eastland (Miss.) Ch.
Constitutional Rights sub-committee	McClellan (Ark.) Ch.
Public Works	Randolph (W. Vir.)

House of Representatives

Appropriations	Mahon (Tex.)
Agriculture sub-committee	Whitten (Miss.)
Defense	Mahon (Tex.)
Foreign Operations	Passman (La.)
Education and Labor	Perkins (Ken.)
Government Operations	Brooks (Tex.)
Interior	Haley (Fl.)
Merchant Marine	Sullivan (Mo.)
Post Office	Henderson (N.C.)
Public Works	Jones (Ala.)
Science	Teague (Tex.)
Small Business	Evins (Tenn.)
Standards of Conduct	Flynt (Ga.)
Veterans	Roberts (Tex.)

* Chairman

It is obvious that the working class movement in the Anglo-American Nation is strangled by the political representatives of Wall Street from the South. There is no way for the Anglo-

American workers to vote these fascists out of office, yet these Southern stooges of Wall Street legislate for the whole USNA. There is but one proper slogan and that is the slogan for a separation of the Negro Nation from the Anglo-American Nation.

In a parallel situation, Marx wrote:

> ...Quite apart from all phrases about 'international' and humane justice for Ireland... it is in the direct and absolute interest of the English working class to get rid of their present connection with Ireland. And this is my fullest conviction, and for reasons which in part I cannot tell the English workers themselves. For a long time, I believed that it would be possible to overthrow the Irish regime by English working class ascendancy. I always expressed this point of view in the *New York Tribune.* Deeper study has now convinced me of the opposite. The English working class will never accomplish anything until it has got rid of Ireland... English reaction in England has its roots in the subjugation of Ireland.(11)

It is from the concrete realities of our political lives, and from the theoretical understanding of a century of struggle against national oppression that we, in the name of the Anglo-American working class demand the independence and freedom of the Negro Nation.

White chauvinism has become a material force—a powerful weapon in the hands of the ruling class to divide the working class, bribe the Anglo-American workers into accepting, if not supporting the aggressive imperialism of the USNA. White chauvinism acts to strengthen the USNA imperialists' oppression and exploitation of the Negro Nation and the Negro national minority. White chauvinism will not be eliminated by simple ideological cleansing campaigns that seek to wash from the minds and bodies of Anglo-American workers such unholy sins as "racism" and "white skin privilege." While we carry on a relentless campaign against white chauvinism in all fields of work, we must deepen our understanding that the necessary material base of white chauvinism is imperialism and white chauvinism will not be completely wiped out until imperialism is defeated. It is from this point of view that within the CLP we project that the concrete fight against white chauvinism is the fight to free the Negro Nation.

White chauvinism can be attacked and defeated in the realm of ideology. In order to succeed, the ideological attack must be linked to the obvious interests of the Anglo-American workers. There can be no unity of the working class without a struggle against white chauvinism. There can be no peace or Socialism without a struggle against white chauvinism. It is entirely possible and necessary to show the Anglo-American working class that the chauvinist bowl of pottage prevents them from achieving the decent, moral and happy life of Socialism.

The objective forces are developing (i.e., the defeats of imperialism) which will tend to unite labor. This unity will be realized if we correctly apply Marxism-Leninism to the solution of the national colonial question in the USNA and the world.

National Cultural Autonomy
Concerning national cultural autonomy Lenin said:

> The gist of this program is that every citizen registers as belonging to a particular nation, and every nation is constituted a legal entity with the right to impose compulsory taxation on its members with national parliaments (diets) and national secretaries of state (ministers).(12)

Although this incorrect approach is manifested in several ways, its primary effect is to divorce the national question from the question of a common and historically evolved territory. Those who put forth the position of national cultural autonomy maintain that the nation is wherever Negro people are living at any given moment. Such formulations generally lead to reformist programs which may have as their goal self-determination (community control), via a parliamentary plebiscite or plea for justice to imperialist institutions like the United Nations or World Court, by ignoring or distorting the question of national territory, the cultural autonomists in the USNA work objectively to preserve the USNA as a multinational imperialist state and encourage class collaboration among all classes within the Negro Nation and among the national minorities. Lenin says of this reactionary theory:

> ...Proudhon was petty-bourgeois, and his theory and programme of 'cultural national autonomy' petty bourgeois for it converts bourgeois nationalism into an absolute category, exalts it as the acme of perfection... Marxism cannot

be reconciled with nationalism be it even of the 'most just,' 'purest' most refined and civilized brand. In place of all forms of nationalism, Marxism advances internationalism, the amalgamation of all nations in higher unity...(13)

Stalin also commented on the divisive effects of this bourgeois theory:

> The idea of national autonomy creates the psychological conditions that make for the division of a united workers' party into separate parties on national lines. The break-up of the party is followed by the break-up of trade unions, and complete isolation is the result. In this way a united class movement is broken up into separate national rivulets.(14)

Within the USNA, national cultural autonomy has also reared us head in the form of a demand that revolutionary parties should be divided along national or "racial" lines. Again it was Stalin who related the Austrian experience to point up further the effects of such a position:

> Let us begin with the 'extremely edifying experience of the Social Democratic Party of Austria.' Up to 1896 there was a united Social Democratic Party of Austria. In that year the Czechs at the International Congress in London for the first time demanded separate representation and were given it. In 1897, at the Vienna (Wimberg) Party Congress, the united Party was formally liquidated and in its place a federal league of six national 'Social Democratic groups' was set up. Subsequently these groups were converted into independent parties which gradually severed contact with one another. Following the parties the parliamentary group also broke up —national 'clubs' were formed. Next came the trade unions, which also split according to nationalities. Even the cooperative societies were affected, the Czech separatists calling upon the workers to split them up. We will not dwell on the fact that separatist agitation weakens the workers' sense of solidarity and frequently drives them to strike-breaking.(15)

Nationalism, expressed as national cultural autonomy, is an expression of bourgeois ideology and must be combated by all honest revolutionaries. On the question of national independence and the fight for democracy, the CLP realizes that the fight for the independence of the Negro Nation will have to be waged primarily among the Anglo-American working class and will have to be one of the major points of the workers' program and practice; on the other hand, the CLP holds the principle of unity of the working class. But the question of unity must be primarily raised by the comrades within the Negro Nation. Lenin clarified this position when he said:

> The weight of emphasis in the internationalist education of the workers in the oppressing countries must necessarily consist of their advocating and upholding freedom of secession of oppressed countries. Without this there can be no internationalism. It is our right and duty to treat every Social Democrat of an oppressing nation who *fails* to conduct such propaganda as an imperialist and a scoundrel. This is an absolute demand, even if the *chance* of secession being possible and 'feasible' before the introduction of socialism be j one in a thousand...
>
> On the other hand, a Social Democrat belonging to a small nation must emphasize in his agitation the *second* word of our general formula: 'voluntary *union*' of nations. He may, without violating his duties as an internationalist, be in favour of *either* the political independence of his nation *or* its inclusion in a neighbouring state X, Y, and Z. But in all cases he must fight against small nations' narrow mindedness, isolationism, and aloofness, he must fight for the recognition of the whole and the general for the subordination of the particular to the interests of the general.
>
> People who have not gone thoroughly into the question think there is a 'contradiction' in Social Democrats of oppressing nations insisting on 'freedom of *secession*,' while Social Democrats of oppressed nations insist on 'freedom of *union*.' However a little reflection will show that there is not and cannot be any *other* road leading from the *given* situation for internationalism and the amalgamation of nations, any other road to this goal.(16)

CHAPTER SEVEN

IMPERIALIST OPPRESSION OF THE NEGRO NATION AND THE SOUTH AS A REGION

In order to uncover and follow the correct path on the Negro national colonial question, it is important to understand the relationship between the Negro Nation and the South as a region.

The South as a region is defined roughly by the area South of the Mason-Dixon line. For statistical purposes the South is usually defined by the government as those 17 states which make up the South-Central and South-Eastern section of the state of the USNA. Within this Southern region lies the Negro Nation with a territory described as the "Black" or "Cotton Belt" area plus the historically and economically connected territory that fringes the Nation. Within the South as a whole live 52% of all the 24 to 30 million Negroes living within the borders of the USNA. Within the Negro Nation live about 10 million people, with the Negro people in the clear majority.

Who Controls the Negro Nation and the South as a Region?

Since the end of the Civil War, the South has been an especially oppressed region of Anglo-America but the oppression of the Black Belt has been that of direct colonial oppression. Since 1870 the South has been controlled economically and politically by Anglo-American monopoly capital, led by the likes of Morgan and Rockefeller. The banks, utilities, timber, railroads, oil, steel, minerals and cash crops were firmly in the hands of the monopoly capitalists by the turn of the century.(1) From then until the present day, the financial institutions of USNA imperialism have continued to consolidate and expand their control over the productive forces and markets of both the Negro Nation and the entire South.

An indication of the extent of finance capital's control over the South as a region was made public on a low level in 1938. The National Emergency Committee in its *Report to the President on Economic Conditions in the South* reported the following:

> Lacking capital of its own the South has been forced to borrow from outside financiers who have reaped a rich harvest in the forms of dividends and interest. At the same time it [independent Southern capital] has had to hand over

the control of much of its business and industry to investors from the wealthier sections. (2)

In its report the committee stated specifically that almost all public works, major railroads, oil, natural gas, iron ore, coal and limestone, bauxite, zinc, sulphur, cotton mills and rayon mills were all owned by "investors" from outside the South.

In 1947, Hodding Carter stated in the *Readers' Digest* that the destruction of independent Southern capital was accomplished with the aid of the age-old principle of colonial empires; lengthy organized cartels which controlled supply, transportation and distribution. In the same year, it was reported that the super-profits of the fertilizer monopoly, operating in the South, were great enough to give a college education to every Southern high school graduate.

Any brief investigation of the economy of the South in general and the Negro Nation in particular will show that the same ruling class cliques which control the majority of the financial institutions and industries in the USNA also control the South. One of the main differences in relation to this financial control is that the imperialist financial power centered around the Rockefeller, Morgan, Mellon and other major bank groupings is, in general, more concentrated in the South than in the USNA as a whole. A good example of this concentrated control can be found in the chemical industry in the South. The chemical industry is big business in that more profits are taken from exploiting the labor of chemical workers than in any other industry within the South. The "value added by manufacture" for the chemical industry was $8½ billion in 1965. (Annual Survey of Manufactures, 1966)

Who owns the giant chemical industry of the South? According to the *Sales Management Directory of Key Plants,* there were 243 plants each employing more than 250 people producing chemical and allied products in 1964. For 220 of these plants additional data is available in *Moody's Industrials.* This data shows that 217 of the 220 plants are controlled directly or indirectly by Anglo-American finance capital. For example, the giants which dominate production in Southern chemicals are Union Carbide (controlled by Manufacturer's Hanover Trust); Monsanto Chemicals (controlled by Chemical Bank of New York, Rockefeller grouping); Allied Chemical (controlled by the Morgan grouping); and, to a lesser extent, the Dow Chemical Company and other holdings of the Du Pont group.

Only about 2% of the chemical plants located in the South are owned by firms which are not connected with the imperialist controlled multinational giants of the chemical industry.

Imperialist control and investment in the Negro Nation and the connected Southern region has brought untold billions of dollars in super-profits to the bloodthirsty directors of high finance. The lower wages and speed-up conditions resulting from the oppression of the Negro colony have produced fantastic super-profits (profits above those taken by capitalists under wage and working conditions prevailing in the Anglo-American Nation). Even a conservative estimate based on such lies as the statistics reported in the *Annual Survey of Manufacturers* indicates that the rate of exploitation in the South as a region is approximately 25-30% higher than in the USNA as a whole.

In addition to the favorable position afforded monopoly capital by discriminatory freight and tariff rates, monopoly control of federal agencies, state legislatures and trade union internationals have produced many tax breaks, lower wage scales, separate labor contracts, and other favorable conditions which dictate super-profits and the domination of Anglo-American businesses in the South.

As the world-wide crisis of capitalism has continued to develop, the imperialists of the USNA have been forced to shift more and more of their industrial base into their colonies and neo-colonies and into the Negro Nation and surrounding territory in particular. The cost of the "shift" of industry into the colonies and neo-colonies, and its continued rapid expansion since W.W. II, has, to a large extent, been born by the working class taxpayers of the USNA. For example, during the recession years of 1949-50 the government of the USNA sponsored the so-called plant decentralization plan under the Defense Mobilizer Program. This program was developed and directed by Charles E. Wilson of the General Electric Company. Essentially, this program provided a $15 billion tax amortization (tax cut) plan which allowed plants to "run away" to the South and resulted in unemployment and a serious weakening of many trade unions in the North. For example, the electrical and garment and textile workers were hard hit.(3)

Imperialist domination and exploitation of the South, as a special region with a total population of about 60 million people, is made possible by the colonial oppression of the Negro Nation – heartland of the South. Combined military power and extra-legal terror have been used by the imperialists to keep the Negro Nation in chains. But to really insure the garrison of the Negro people and expanding colonial super-profits, the South as a region, with its large Negro national minority, must also be divided along national and class lines. It must also be subjected to nearly the same kind of fascist political and economic oppression that is concentrated in the Negro Nation. As long as the Negro Nation remains in chains, the Southern working class as a whole will of necessity suffer a somewhat similar fate.

Later in this section we will compare concretely the oppression and exploitation of the Negro workers and toilers with that of their Anglo-American and Negro national minority counterparts living outside the probable area of the Nation but inside the South. But the impact of Negro national oppression and the resulting imperialist domination of the South on the Anglo-American working class must also be examined.

First of all, it is clear that the low wages paid to Negro national and southern workers act as a direct drag on the wages of workers employed in the same industries in the Anglo-American Nation. Workers in the "North" can't improve their wages too much when the corporation can get more work done for less at a Southern-based plant. Further, Anglo-American workers in many industries constantly face the threat that the company will "run away" to the South if the workers don't tone down their demands for higher wages and better working conditions.

In addition, Anglo-American workers must realize the imperialists have always used the "army of unemployed" or "reserve labor force" in the Anglo-American Nation to break strikes, hold wages down and force speed-up conditions in nearly every sector of the economy. This reserve force in the Anglo-American Nation has traditionally been reinforced by the giant reserve force of low-paid, unemployed and job-hungry workers in the Negro Nation and in the South. Just recall the large number of workers recruited from these areas for the purpose of holding wages down during past periods of war time and rapid economic expansion.

The oppression of the Negro Nation effects Anglo-American workers adversely in many ways. For instance, much progressive legislation has been blocked and many anti-working class laws and decisions have been made by the U.S. Congress under the direction of the fascist, white chauvinist, southern Congressmen, who are

106

agents of USNA imperialism. Congressmen like Stennis, Eastland, Fulbright and others stand on the backs of the Negro people and oppose the interests of the working class of the USNA.

The above facts describe only some of the ways the Anglo-American working class is held back in the struggle for a socialist revolution by the oppression of the Negro Nation. It should be evident to all class-conscious workers in the USNA that the working class in this country cannot unite and take any real steps forward in the organized struggle against fascist USNA imperialism until the demand for an independent Negro Nation is raised and recognized through action.

Recognizing the Differences Between the Negro Nation and the South as a Region

Despite the similar forms of oppression found in the Negro Nation and the South as a whole, there are important differences in the living conditions or levels of oppression which set the Negro Nation apart from the South as a region. For example, voter registration in the 17 Southern states for the 1972 presidential election totaled 24,707,000 Anglo-Americans and 4,386,000 Negroes; while 64% of the Negro national population in the South is of voting age as opposed to 70% of Southern Anglo-Americans.(4) In the seven Southern states which contain the bulk of the Negro Nation (Black Belt and connected areas) the average number of eligible Negroes registered to vote was only 29.6%. In the remaining 10 states generally considered part of the South the average number of eligible Negroes registered to vote was over 50%.(5)

These differences in voter registration would have been greater had only "Black Belt" counties been used in calculating the relative percentages. It should also be noted that while total voter registration has increased greatly since the "freedom movement" of the sixties, the relative differences between the "Black Belt" area of the Negro Nation and the rest of the South still remain.

Reported Voter Registration for Persons of Voting Age, by Region: 1968 and 1972

(Numbers in thousands)

Subject	Presidential Elections			
	Black		White	
	1968	1972	1968	1972
All persons of voting age:				
United States	10,935	13,494	104,521	121,241
South	5,991	6,950	28,834	35,411
North and West	4,944	6,544	75,687	85,830
Number who reported they registered:				
United States	7,238	8,836	78,835	88,896
South	3,690	4,449	20,416	24,701
North and West	3,548	4,386	58,419	64,278
Percent of voting-age population:				
United States	66	65	75	73
South	62	64	71	70
North and West	72	67	77	75

Source: U.S. Department of Commerce, Social and Economic Statistics Administration Bureau of the Census.

Some additional data which shows roughly the same differences as those cited above deals with income levels in the South as a whole as opposed to the seven state area encompassing most of the Negro Nation. Within the Negro Nation, the combined median income of Negro families and Anglo-American minority was about $6,565 per year. The same combined statistics for the Negro national minority and Anglo-American families in the five states which border the Negro Nation was $6,838 per year. Again, the difference would have been greater had more precise statistics been available.(6) It should i also be added that the median income of families in the South as a whole was considerably lower than the State of the

USNA as a whole. In the North, Anglo-American families averaged $12,004 per year, while Negro national minority families averaged only $8,109. In the South (including 17 states) Anglo-American families averaged $10,465 and Negro families averaged $5,763 per year.(7) These differing income levels reflect in a distinct way the level of economic oppression in the Negro Nation relative to the South as a region and the USNA as a whole.

MEDIAN INCOME OF FAMILIES:
1950-1972

(In current dollars)

| Year | Race of head of family | | |
	Negro & other races	Negro	White
1950	$1,869	(NA)	$3,445
1955	2,549	(NA)	4,605
1960	3,233	(NA)	5,835
1965	3,994	$3,886	7,251
1970	6,516	6,279	10,236
1971	6,714	6,440	10,672
1972			
United States	7,106	6,864	11,549
South	5,730	5,763	10,465
North and West	8,604	8,109	12,004
Northeast	7,984	7,816	12,307
North Central	8,574	8,318	11,947
West	9,434	8,313	11,724

Source: U.S. Department of Commerce, Social and Economic Statistics Administration, Bureau of the Census.

The status of organized labor further confirms the colonial position of the Negro Nation. Again, in the seven states containing the greater part of the Negro Nation, the percentage of the non-agricultural labor force belonging to unions in 1964 was about 14.2%. In the remaining 10 states which are considered part of the South, the percentage was about 24% while the figure for all 50 states was about

27.8%.(8) Other statistics showing the difference in educational levels, percentage of sub-standard housing, infant mortality rates, number of political assassinations and extra-legal executions all further confirm the real differences which exist between the Negro Nation and the South, on the one hand, and the South and the USNA as a whole on the other.

Although the Negro and Anglo-American toilers and workers of the Southern region are struggling for freedom, equal rights and a de cent life, the political solution for that area which will emerge as a result of the struggle of the Negro Nation must of necessity differ from the political solutions that will be possible for the Negro Nation. The South as a region does not have the concrete potential for emerging as an independent nation exercising the right to self-determination, but the Negro Nation definitely does.

MEASURES OF INCOME IN 1967 AND 1972 OF FAMILIES, BY TYPE OF FAMILY AND REGION

(In current dollars)

Subject	Median income		
	Negro	White	Ratio Negro to White
1967			
All families	$4,875	$8,234	0.59
Region:			
South	3,953	7,359	0.54
Northeast	5,644	8,659	0.65
North Central	6,402	8,350	0.77
West	6,511	8,808	0.74
Type of family:			
Male head	5,737	8,557	0.67
Wife in paid labor force	7,272	10,196	0.71
Wife not in paid labor force	4,662	7,743	0.60
Female head	3,004	4,855	0.62
1972			
All families	$6,864	$11,549	0.59
Region			
South	5,763	10,465	0.55
Northeast	7,816	12,307	0.64
North Central	8,318	11,947	0.70
West	8,313	11,724	0.71
Type of family:			
Male head	9,037	12,102	0.75
Wife in paid labor force	11,336	14,148	0.80
Wife not in paid labor force	6,900	10,806	0.64
Female head	3,840	6,213	0.62

Source: U.S. Department of Commerce, Social and Economic Statistics Administration Bureau of the Census.

WHITE FAMILIES, FAMILIES OF NEGRO AND OTHER RACES, BY TOTAL MONEY INCOME IN CONSTANT 1967 DOLLARS: 1947 to 1968

Income	1968	1965	1960	1955	1950	1947
WHITE FAMILIES						
Number — thousands	45,437	43,497	41,123	38,982	(NA)	34,120
Percent	100.0	100.0	100.0	100.0	100.0	100.0
Under $3,000	9.6	12.8	16.4	19.4	25.0	24.1
$3,000 to $4,999	11.7	13.5	16.5	20.7	28.4	30.4
$5,000 to $6,999	15.3	17.3	21.6	24.0	22.4	21.8
$7,000 to $9,999	24.7	25.5	24.1	22.1	15.3	14.2
$10,000 to $14,999	24.0	20.8	15.0	10.2	9.0	9.5
$15,000 and over	14.9	10.0	6.2	3.5		
Median Income — dollars	9,589	7,670	6,601	5,766	4,796	4,720
FAMILIES OF NEGRO AND OTHER RACES						
Number — thousands	5,074	4,954	4,333	3,907	(NA)	(NA)
Percent	100.0	100.0	100.0	100.0	100.0	100.0
Under $3,000	24.5	33.0	42.0	47.5	57.7	62.4
$3,000 to $4,999	22.1	25.0	23.1	27.2	29.1	22.3
$5,000 to $6,999	16.7	16.5	15.9	14.5	8.0	7.9
$7,000 to $9,999	17.7	14.7	11.9	8.6	3.5	5.1
$10,000 to $14,999	13.1	8.7	5.8	1.7	1.8	2.2
$15,000 and over	5.9	2.0	1.3	0.3		
Median income — dollars	5,377	4,256	3,644	3,185	2,591	2,418

NEGROES AS A PERCENT OF TOTAL WAGE AND SALARY WORKERS, BY INDUSTRY, AND LABOR UNION MEMBERSHIP, 1970

Industry of longest job held	Total wage & salary workers		In labor unions		Not in unions	
	Number (1000s)	% Negro	Number (1000s)	% Negro	Number (1000s)	% Negro
All Industries	84,256	11.6	17,192	12.4	67,063	11.4
Mining	574	4.4	205	4.9	368	4.3
Construction	4,975	10.2	1,948	8.7	3,027	11.2
Manufacturing, total	22,503	10.7	7,600	12.4	14,903	9.8
Transportation, communication and public utilities	5,642	10.7	2,527	10.3	3,115	11.1
Wholesale trade	3,047	8.1	345	11.9	2,701	7.6
Retail trade	13,732	8.0	1,363	9.7	12,368	7.9
Services and finance	27,115	13.9	2,103	18.6	25,012	13.5
Public administration	4,761	12.8	1,055	16.5	3,706	11.8

Source: Selected Earnings and Demographic Characteristics of Union Membership, 1970 Report 417, U. S. Department of Labor, Bureau of Labor Statistics

LABOR UNION MEMBERSHIP RATES, BY REGION, INDUSTRY, SEX, AND RACE, 1970

Percent in labor unions

Industry of longest job held in 1970 and sex	Northeast			North Central			South			West		
	All races	White	Negro and other	All races	White	Negro and other	All races	White	Negro and other	All races	White	Negro and other
Both sexes												
All industries	25.0	24.1	34.2	25.6	24.8	35.7	11.4	11.4	11.4	20.8	20.4	25.4
Agriculture	5.6	5.5	(2)	1.0	1.0	(2)	.4	.7		5.6	5.2	(2)
Mining	54.2	53.1	(2)	52.9	52.9	(2)	22.5	21.8	(2)	42.5	43.2	(2)
Construction	46.3	45.3	(2)	48.8	48.4	(2)	22.2	23.2	17.4	51.0	50.2	(2)
Manufacturing, total	37.3	36.6	46.4	43.8	42.1	64.8	20.5	19.5	24.9	28.7	28.2	34.2
Transportation, communication and public utilities	49.7	49.7	49.7	52.4	52.2	54.6	32.1	32.5	30.0	48.1	47.0	57.3
Trade, total	13.3	12.5	27.4	11.2	10.7	20.2	3.6	3.4	4.8	15.1	15.2	13.7
Services and finance	11.2	10.1	20.8	8.5	7.9	14.3	2.9	2.7	3.8	9.6	8.9	16.1
Public administration	31.4	29.3	50.9	24.8	24.0	29.9	12.8	12.6	14.4	23.4	22.3	30.4
Male												
All industries	31.7	31.0	39.8	35.3	34.4	47.3	16.5	16.4	17.1	28.7	28.3	33.0
Female												
All industries	15.5	14.2	27.8	12.1	11.2	22.0	4.7	4.6	5.1	10.2	9.5	17.0

(2) Base less than 75,000

Source: Selected Earnings and Demographic Characteristics of Union Members, 1970. Report 417.
U.S Department of Labor, Bureau of Labor Statistics

114

MATERNAL AND INFANT MORTALITY RATES: 1940, 1950, 1960, 1970, 1971

(per 1,000 live births)

| Year | Negro and other races | | White | |
	Maternal	Infant under 1 yr.	Maternal	Infant under 1 yr.
1940	7.6	73.8	3.2	43.2
1950	2.2	44.5	0.6	26.8
1960	1.0	43.2	0.3	22.9
1970	(NA)	31.4	(NA)	17.4
1971	(NA)	30.2	(NA)	16.8

Source: U.S. Department of Health, Education, and Welfare,
National Center for Health Statistics

Specifically on the question of how the national colonial question will be handled in relation to the Southern Negroes living inside the likely territory or borders of the Negro Nation, the position put forward by Charles P. Mann in his 1954 pamphlet *Stalin's Thought Illuminates Problems of Negro Freedom Struggle* remains essentially sound:

> Generally speaking we would say that the large Negro minorities who live in the South but outside of the likely borders of the territory of the Negro Nation must be viewed as a part of or extensions of, the Negro Nation. We must stress the point, however, that we are obliged in each instance to examine the particular, concrete relationship and the extent of the common ties that each 'removed' community of the Negroes has to the national base. Is it not obvious that the Negro community in Atlanta, Ga., a city beyond the probable boundary lines of the Negro Nation's territory— for example, would and does have more binding and extensive connections with the Negro Nation than say the 'Negro' community of Hartford, Conn.?

> Moreover, a large part of the Negro industrial working class of the South is located in these communities, and the leading role of this class within the Negro national liberation movement, is of basic importance.

> Though the several respective Negro minority communities in the South may put to the fore one or another point

of the full program of the Negro national liberation movement, all of these communities are in need of, would fight for, and would directly benefit from any gains won on the road to freedom by the Negro Nation.

In order to correctly understand and organize the national and class struggles in the Negro Nation and the South as a region, we should always keep in mind Stalin's instructions to the communists working in the border regions of the Soviet Union when he indicated they "must unfailingly take into account all the peculiarities of economic life, class structure, and historical past which mark the regions.(9)

In front of their three-room house in Mississippi sit three children and their mother, who finished only seventh grade in school; the house has no running water, electricity, or inside toilet facilities.
Source: Ebony Magazine, Vol. 26, No. 10, August, 1971

CHAPTER EIGHT

THE NEGRO NATIONAL MINORITY IN THE ANGLO-AMERICAN NATION

The Negro national minority in the Anglo-American Nation is made up of those 11 million Negroes living outside the Black Belt area of the Negro Nation and the immediately surrounding area of the South. This Negro national minority, which includes more than one million Negroes who have migrated within the last generation, is concentrated for the most part in less than 20 major urban centers of the Anglo-American Nation, particularly in the East and the industrial belt extending from Pittsburg through Chicago. Approximately three-fourths of the Negro national minority either migrated from the Negro Nation or were born in the North before 1945. The majority of the Negroes living in the Anglo-American territory of the State of the USNA still have blood ties in the South.

The millions of Negroes who were born in the Negro Nation, but who have migrated North, did so in an attempt to escape the starvation, low wages and fascist rule in the Negro colony. Often Negroes were lured to the North by unscrupulous labor recruiters who were paid "by the head" for strong bodies sent to company towns or labor camps. This was particularly true during the period from 1900 to 1910 and again from 1917 to 1924, when nearly 3 million Negroes migrated to the North. For example, during the period from 1907 to 1928, when the United Mine Workers were organizing the coal fields in West Virginia, Kentucky, southern Illinois and elsewhere, tens of thousands of Negro workers were recruited from the Negro Nation for the purpose of driving wages down and breaking strikes.

> The United Mine Workers were unable to organize the mines of southern W. Virginia due in part to the large supply of redundant Negro labor brought in from the South. The existence of such a store of labor has given to the operators in W. Virginia, and in practically every other mining section of the country, an industrial reserve army which may be used either to defeat the purposes of unionism or to meet an increased demand for labor caused by the expansion of industry.(1)

The demand for labor from the Negro Nation became particularly great after the source of USNA capitalism's cheap immigrant labor was cut off by the advent of World War I. During the years 1916 through 1924, millions of Negroes migrated North. Many were tricked into migrating by false promises of a better life. During 1916 and 1917, the Illinois Central Railroad recruited and dumped some 10,000 Negro workers into East St. Louis in order to drive the going wage down for the track-laying labor hired in that town. This maneuver by the capitalists forced people to sleep in the streets and wages fell to new lows. These conditions and provocations by Illinois Central agents, who pitted Anglo-American against Negro national minority workers ignited the "race riot" of 1917 in which scores of Negro national minority workers were killed and hundreds injured.

The gradual outcome of the monopoly capitalists' policy toward the Negro national minority and "fresh" Negro immigrant workers was their inclusion as more or less permanent workers in the basic industries of Anglo-America. By 1920 between 20 and 40% of the workers employed in meat-packing, steel, auto, and chemicals were Negro national minority. By 1928, the number of Negro national minority workers employed in the basic manufacturing, mining and transportation industries numbered nearly two million.

These Negro national minority workers had jobs but they were at the bottom of the skills pile, with 95% of these two million jobs classified as unskilled and low paying. Yet another indication of the low status of Negro national minority workers was the relatively small number of those organized as opposed to unorganized. By 1928 only about 56,000 of the nearly 2 million Negro national minority industrial workers in the Anglo American Nation were union members. Even when a Negro national minority worker managed to slip into a skilled job, he was paid less than his Anglo-American working-class counterpart. For example, in 1928, Negro railroad engineers were paid $4.71 per 100 freight miles, while Anglo-American engineers were paid $5.75 for the same work.(2)

From 1870 to the 1930's, the workers of the Negro Nation were driven from the plantations to the factories, mills and mines, where daily they risked their lives as the lowest paid of all minority workers. Those who could not find work became part of the reserve labor force of big capital—the Rockefellers, Morgans, Fords, Carnegies, all used the weapon of white chauvinism to drive Negro national minority workers to the wall. This tactic of divide-and-conquer has cost the lives and limbs of millions of the working class. Both Negro and Anglo-American workers suffered from the poor working conditions and low pay promoted by class division.

It was this division of the working class that held back the entire labor movement and slowed the organizing of the industrial unions. An example of the divisive strategy practiced by the imperialist rulers can be seen in a comment made by a top official of the Carnegie Steel Company in 1928. He stated:

> We employ about 10% Negroes in our plant and we could get along without them. However, we do not choose to do so, since a cosmopolitan labor force makes fraternizing among the employees difficult.(3)

During the latter part of the 1930's, the Negro national minority j joined enthusiastically in the labor and other progressive movements of the day. Constantly struggling for their equal rights and fighting every step of the way for trade unions, Negro national minority workers were often in the front lines of the battle. Many advanced workers built organizations such as the National Negro Congress (1936) to fight for the rights of Negro workers and the freedom of the Negro Nation, and joined with the Communist Party in organizing Unemployed Councils. However, it was not until 1937-38, when the big drive to organize the Committee for Industrial Organizations was launched, that Negro national minority workers of the Anglo-American Nation were really drawn in large numbers into the organized labor movement. Membership of Negro national minority workers in unions jumped from about 110,000 in 1930 to about 759,000 at the end of World War II. By 1950, about 1.5 million Negro workers (mostly in the Anglo-American Nation) were in trade unions.(4)

Although the Negro national minority worker was drawn more and more into the heart of Anglo-American industry between 1930 and 1950, this was due only in part to the efforts of the CIO and the Communist Party. More important forces operating were World War II and the resulting rapid expansion and mechanization of industry, and the growing monopoly concentration. As Marx pointed out in the *Communist Manifesto:*

In proportion, therefore, as the repulsiveness of the work increases, the wage decreases. Nay more, in proportion as the use of machinery and division of labor increases, in the same proportion the burden of toil increases, whether by prolongation of working hours, by increases of work exacted in a given time, or by increased speed of the machinery...(5)

In short, Negro national minority workers were pulled into industry to do the jobs no one else would do under the speed-up conditions and poor wages the capitalists were offering.

To the present day, contrary to what capitalists of all nationalities say, the Negro national minority worker has not improved his position relative to the non-minority member of the Anglo-American working class. Neither has the Negro national minority worker been integrated or accepted as an equal, despite the actions of the NAACP, the Urban League, Equal Rights Commission, et. al. As proof, consider the Negro national minority workers' unemployment situation: In 1959, 24% of national minority workers were unemployed as against 14.2% Anglo-American. In 1964, there was very little change and that for the worse. 25.5% of Negro national minority workers were unemployed against 15% Anglo-American. By May 12, 1975, 14.6% of the Negro national minority workers were unemployed against 8.1% Anglo-American.

Look also at comparable wage data. Since World War II, Negro national minority workers on the average have received only about one-half the annual wage paid to Anglo-American labor. Negro national minority workers on the average have earned 13% less than Anglo-Americans for the same work.(6) Or further, consider the position of Negro national minority workers in skilled or white collar jobs. In the Chicago Civil Service Region, 19% of all employees are Negro national minority workers, but 27% of all workers at the lowest pay levels are Negro national minority workers.(7) Finally, a recent study done in Chicago showed that after more than 100 years in the job market the Negro national minority worker "is still confined to certain sectors of the labor market."(8)

These facts, reflecting discrimination, oppression and exploitation suffered by the Negro national minority workers of Anglo-America are endless, just as the super-profits the monopoly capitalists have made off their labor are countless.

UNEMPLOYMENT RATES BY AGE, SEX, AND RACE: 1955-1972

(Annual Averages)

	16 to 19 years old				20 years old and			
	White		Negro & other races		White		Negro & other races	
	Male	Female	Male	Female	Male	Female	Male	Female
1955	11.3	9.1	13.4	19.2	3.3	3.9	8.4	7.7
1960	14.0	12.7	24.0	24.8	4.2	4.6	9.6	8.3
1965	12.9	14.0	23.3	31.7	2.9	4.0	6.0	7.5
1970	13.7	13.4	25.0	34.4	3.2	4.4	5.6	6.9
1972	14.2	14.2	29.7	38.5	3.6	4.9	6.8	8.8

Source: Bureau of Labor Statistics, Employment & Earnings, Vol. 19, No. 8.

UNEMPLOYMENT RATES, BY EDUCATIONAL ATTAINMENT: 1965-1972

By Age and Race

Year	Total			White			Negro & other races		
	Under 12 yrs.	12 Yrs.	Over 12 yrs.	Under 12 yrs.	12 Yrs.	Over 12 yrs.	Under 12 yrs.	12 Yrs.	Over 12 yrs.
Age 18 & Over									
1965	6.6	4.1	2.3	5.9	3.7	2.3	9.8	8.2	2.4
1970	5.6	3.9	2.7	3.6	2.6	7.3	7.3	7.1	4.0
1972	7.3	5.5	3.7	6.6	5.1	3.5	10.6	9.6	6.5
Ages 18-34									
1972	13.4	7.7	5.0	11.7	7.0	4.9	20.4	13.0	6.8

Source: Bureau of Labor Statistics, unpublished data.

As we have demonstrated, the Negro national minority in the Anglo-American Nation has suffered more than a century of oppression and hardship. The vast working class and poor sections of the Negro national minority have responded to these conditions with growing militancy that has been expressed in many strike actions, protest movements, and armed uprisings against the State of the USNA. Although the root of the majority of these protest movements and freedom struggles can be traced to the Negro Nation, the strike waves and spontaneous armed uprisings have occurred on a much broader scale in the North than within the Negro Nation. At least this was true for the decade just ended.

This is explained from several points of view. First and most important, the concentrations of Negro national minorities in such cities as Cleveland, Los Angeles, Chicago, and New York are unknown in the South. Therefore, the communications and sweep of mass sentiment cannot take place on the same level. Also, the compromised classes in the South have a much firmer hold on the Negro masses than in the North. These related reasons have held the breadth of the movement in check. Also, the Negro national minority faces a different kind of oppression than the open fascist terror that rules the Negro Nation. Nevertheless, it should be noted that every wave of struggle has had its beginnings in the Negro Nation.

The Negro national minority was for a time able to arise in a spontaneous manner to oppose the police and the imperialist state. These spontaneous uprisings, which shook the foundations of the state of the USNA, hit their peak in 1965-1968.

The USNA imperialists have moved rapidly to clamp a lid on the movement; to tighten their fascist oppression. Elaborate battle plans have been drawn up and in some cases put into action against the industrial slave quarters where the majority of the Negro national minority workers reside. Police departments have increased their armed attacks on Negro national minority working class communities; thousands of new intelligence agents and provocateurs have been sent into minority communities; the flow of heroin and other hard drugs to minority communities has been stepped up; attempts to bribe "community leaders" have increased and phony plans for "community control" by the Negro national minority community abound.

As the class and national colonial contradictions have heightened within the world and within the State of the USNA, the imperialist ruling class has been forced more and more in the direction of imposing upon the Anglo-American working class the same type of fascist rule that has long existed in the Negro Nation. This fascist counter-revolution is advancing "legally" and under the cloak of

122

law and order, because such a fascist rule has for decades legally existed in the Negro Nation. Wage controls, gun laws, unlawful assembly, conspiracy and all such laws are simply rewritten from the existing statutes of the Negro Nation. The move toward fascism in the Anglo-American Nation is, to a great extent, the result of the struggles of the colonial world and especially the Negro Nation.

To summarize the question of the Negro national minority in the Anglo-American Nation: they have been forced into social production where they live by the objective economic laws that determine social organization. Negro national minority workers hold a large number of jobs in the basic industries and they are an integral part of the Anglo-American working class.

Negro national minority workers hold a high percentage of the most unstable, hazardous, hot and heavy jobs in the economy due to their major role in the reserve labor force and their systematic exclusion from skilled jobs. The majority of Negro national minority workers are forced to perform this undesirable labor in order to feed their families and stay out of the concentration camps that are mislabeled reformatories and penitentiaries, (e.g., the Negro national minority is 6% of the California population and makes up nearly 40% of the California prison population, with Mexican national minorities making up almost the rest of the prison population.)

The oppression of a national minority living in the imperialist country is, by no means, the exclusive plight of the Negro national minority. On the contrary, the special oppression and super-exploitation of the national minority is an inevitable link in the imperialist chain. Such oppression and exploitation flows with the capitalist system. The workers of the oppressed nations come to the imperialist countries poverty racked, often in ill health, unable to speak the language, poorly educated and often of an alien religious background or different color. Capitalists cannot fail to recognize that such immigrants are especially vulnerable and defenseless. The national minorities become locked in the slums that are their first homes, the differences between them and the peoples of the imperialist countries are institutionalized.

Simultaneously with the rise of profits is the rationalization and systematization of the "theories" of the inferiority and separateness of these "outsiders." With the Irish national minority residing in England this special and super-exploitation of the Irish national minority took place first by concentration on language and cultural difference, and as these faded away, the religious question became the focal point. For the Irish, this religious factor became the only possible battle ground in the struggle for equality. This religious factor is ever present in the relations between Irish and English. This weapon of oppression—the religious struggle—was inherited from the specifics of history.

There is nothing in the history of the Negro people and their relationship with the Anglo-American Nation to inject a religious factor. The factor in the USNA that made simple the continued super-exploitation of the Negro national minority was the color factor.

The capitalist wants to prevent the real integration of the Negro national minority into the Anglo-American Nation for the same reason that the English capitalists want to prevent the integration of the Irish national minority or the Japanese capitalists want to prevent the integration of the Korean national minority. That reason is super-profits and the method of operation is the same. The color factor, inherited from history, becomes a real weapon in continuing and increasing the oppression, segregation and exploitation of the Negro national minority. It appears that indeed the state anthem of Kentucky speaks the truth, "For the back must bend and the head will have to bow, wherever the Darky may go."

The special oppression of the Negro national minority also serves another important purpose. It acts as a stopper or a brake on any dangerous out migration from the Negro Nation. "Since things aren't that much better in Detroit than in Birmingham—it's better to stay here where there is at least a home and loved ones." Further, the special oppression and exploitation of the Negro national minority reinforces white chauvinism, institutionalizes the divisions in the working class by making the bribe to the Anglo-American workers dearer and facilitates an alliance between the Anglo-American workers and capitalists in the exploitation of the Negro Nation and the whole of the colonial world.

Because they cannot be fully integrated, the Negro national minority workers have remained over many generations culturally, politically and "spiritually" linked with "their people" who inhabit the Negro Nation. At the same time, brutal oppression and second-class citizenship have forced the Negro national minority workers to realize that the fight for freedom in the Negro Nation is their fight, and the future of the Negro Nation will largely determine their own. In addition, the position in the working class of the Negro national minority workers has forced them to become part of the most class conscious and revolutionary element within the Anglo-American Nation. Thus, the Negro national minority worker, by virtue of his ties with the Negro Nation and position within the Anglo-American working class provides the concrete link between the Negro people and the Anglo-American working class. Moreover, the Negro national minority not only objectively links the Anglo-American workers to the Negro Nation—but through the Negro Nation to the whole of the colonial world. Thus, the Negro national minority plays a key role in completing the encirclement of USNA imperialism by the fighting colonial masses. Indeed, the vanguard Negro national minority workers provide the basis for the unity of struggle between the Anglo-American working class for their emancipation and the Negro Nation for liberation. One struggle cannot proceed without the other.

So we see that the colonial position of the Negro Nation, while holding back the struggle of the Anglo-American working class in many ways that have already been pointed out, is also a major force that propels not only the Negro national minority but the entire Anglo-American working class forward in the life and death struggle against imperialism of the USNA.

The long history of labor's struggle in the USNA points up the fact that there is only one road for Negro and Anglo-American workers: the fight for the unity of the working class. The Communist Labor Party sees the long and bloody history of white chauvinism and the "color" divisions that have dominated the landscape of USNA history as the concrete expressions of the profound and fundamental class and national contradictions within the State of the USNA. The attempts of the ruling class to maintain a division of the working class through the use of chauvinist bribery, force and violence, as well as by extending petty bribes and privileges, has already been doomed to failure by the anti-imperialist struggles of the Asian, African and Latin American allies of the Negro people.

All communists and progressive-minded people must now carry forward the ideological struggle for clarity on the Negro National Colonial question in the USNA and to demand by concrete action: Equal Rights for the Negro national minority! Independence for the Negro Nation!

CHAPTER NINE

THE ANGLO-AMERICAN MINORITY
IN THE NEGRO NATION

Within the general territory which makes up the Negro Nation, a majority of the population is made up of Negro men and women. In the territorial core of the Negro Nation—that is, the Black Belt—there is a continuous stretch of overwhelming Negro majority. However, as Lenin stated:

> But the national composition of the population is one of the most important economic factors, *not the only one and not the most important.* Towns for example, play a most important economic role under capitalism.... To separate the towns from the villages and areas which economically gravitate toward them for the sake of the 'national factor' would be absurd and impossible. Marxists therefore must not take their stand entirely and exclusively on the 'national territorial' principle.(1)

History and economic development have absolutely linked the destinies of the surrounding area with the Black Belt. Therefore, we see that a large minority of the people of the Negro Nation are Anglo-American. Because of imperialist terror and bribery, the power of white chauvinist ideology and the resulting separate lines of social development forced upon the Negro people and Anglo-American minority members of the Negro Nation, the common historical development of all the people of the Negro Nation has been obscured. Slavery was a system that involved more than the African slave. That African slave was the base of slavery just as the Negro people are the base of the Negro Nation. The slave system involved a number of Anglo-European and Indian slaves and, of course, the non-slave elements who made their living serving slavery in some capacity—or hacking out a living along side it. The point is that the Negro Nation's roots lie in the basis of the slave system, and cannot help but involve those people who were in some way involved with that system. So-called color differences have been emphasized by the reactionary forces of the USNA imperialists to prevent the development of a united revolutionary national movement for the liberation of the Negro Nation and the establishment of socialism.

The Anglo-American minority of the Nation can be roughly divided into three major sections: first, the toiling, poverty-wracked elements that trace their history back for generations as proletarians, independent farmers and tenant farmers. Second, there are the homegrown petty capitalists (Anglo-American) and phony politicians. A third and less prominent section of the Anglo-American minority consists of those petty bourgeois and bribed working class elements that constitute the real social base of the white chauvinist, imposter politicians and other Wall Street front men.

The first, or toiling proletarian element, is by far the largest and most important segment of the Anglo-American minority. A real struggle must be waged to unite this oppressed Anglo-American minority with the Negro vanguard of the proletariat in the struggle for Negro national liberation and socialism.

Many so-called revolutionaries and upstanding progressives in the Anglo-American Nation deny the many examples of outstanding proletarian and anti-imperialist fighters that have emerged in times past, and are emerging today from the ranks of the Anglo-American minority.

These enemies of the Negro people point solely to the role played by the Anglo-American minority as the ever present "jailers" of the Negro people for the Anglo-American imperialists. That aspect of the Anglo-American minority's development—the field bosses, prison guards, foremen, informers, sheriffs, KKK members and other tools of oppression—cannot be denied. In fact, it was to a degree this role that made them part of the Negro Nation. But we must realize that the hiring of these tools of oppression and the chauvinist divisions within the Negro Nation, have been made possible not by the low level, but real bribery of the Anglo-American minority workers in relation to the Negroes. By bribed, we mean that the Anglo-American workers of the Nation have in general received a few more of the bare necessities of life, and more social rights and privileges than their Negro brothers and sisters. A quick glance at any statistics reflecting living conditions will quickly confirm this fact. This bribery has consisted in the main of a few more crumbs provided by imperialist exploitation of the Negro people. As imperialism is defeated, so is the material base for the bribery of the working and toiling Anglo-American minority of the Negro Nation.

(Right) An assembly line at the International Harvester plant in Louisville, Kentucky, where Negroes and Anglo-Americans work together.

Anglo-American and Negro women workers on the shop floor.
Source: Langston Hughes & Milton Meltzer, A Pictorial History of the Negro in America (New York: Crown Publishers, Inc., 1956).

128

The poverty of the Anglo-American minority in the Negro Nation is, in spite of the bribe, a direct result of the colonial position of the Negro people and Nation. Imperialism has constructed the social relations between the Anglo-American minority and the Negro people so that it often appears that it is the Anglo-American minority who is the oppressor and exploiter of the Negro people rather than the social, economic and political relationships of imperialism. During the period of slavery the economic and social well-being of the Anglo-American minority was dependent upon the position of the Negro majority. This is just as true today as a hundred years ago. This intertwined history has bound class brothers and sisters of different nationalities together and molded them through periods of antagonism and cooperation into a single nationality with a single destiny.

The common history is far too long to recount, but in addition to the facts already mentioned, some of the realities which show the common background in the Negro Nation are: Both Negroes and Anglo-Americans were slaves (Anglo-Americans were generally indentured rather than chattel slaves) in the earliest days of the plantation system. Both Negroes and Anglo-Americans were subjected to centuries of oppression and hardships relative to the workers in the Anglo-American Nation. Many Anglo-American toilers were slaughtered along with their "freed" Negro brothers in the Reconstruction struggles for land and freedom. The post-reconstruction years, the Populist Movement and later World War I saw numerous examples of cooperation between ex-slaves and Anglo-American toilers.(2) During strikes by the Brotherhood of Timberworkers in 1912 and throughout the United Mine Workers organizing drive in the Negro Nation, which involved militant strikes in 1904, 1908, 1917 and I 1920, Negro and Anglo-American workers battled the imperialists together in united unions until they were finally beaten back by the open fascist terror of the KKK and the USNA government. In the 1920's and 1930's there was further cooperation in organizing sharecroppers unions and the CIO and massive Unemployed Councils which grew up throughout the South under the leadership of brave fighters.(3) More recent times have seen increased unity between Negro and Anglo-American workers in the ship and building construction industries, hospital industry, and other struggles where the working class is beginning to feel more and more the raw edge of fascism.

Hard times and the threat of extermination have promoted unified action between Negro and Anglo-American workers before, and hard times are leading in the same direction today. But the struggle for national liberation and socialism requires more than spontaneous cooperation based on a common desperation or reformist battles which lead into one blind alley after another. It will require a high degree of class consciousness and internationalism on the part of both the Negro majority and the Anglo-American minority in the Negro Nation. This consciousness can only be built around a united struggle for Negro National Independence that is closely linked with the fight for socialism in the Negro Nation and the USNA as a whole.

Unlike the Negro people, these members of the Anglo-American minority who migrate from the Negro Nation are usually integrated into Anglo-American society within a generation or two. The previously described color factor in the USNA prevents the integration of the Negro national minority. Through the use of this color factor, no Negro toiler can gain equal rights or real freedom. However, under these circumstances, USNA imperialism cannot prevent the escape of the Anglo-American minority nor too much hinder their assimilation into Anglo-America. This integration is not a simple matter for these workers. They must rapidly exchange their folk ways and idiomatic expressions for those of Anglo-America. More and more they have been returning to the South after a bitter taste of no jobs and hard times slum life. There has been many a verse written like those in the song *Detroit City* which describes the hard life and deep isolation suffered by the Anglo-American minority from the Negro Nation in their struggle to integrate themselves into the Anglo-American Nation.

CHAPTER TEN

CONCLUSION

We are living in the historic era of moribund capitalism—imperialism. We live in the decades of imperialist wars and proletarian revolutions, the era marked by the transition of nations and peoples from capitalism to socialism. The question of developing an international front of struggle of the working class becomes a fundamental question in the tactics of the class. The questions of maneuver and reserves become basic questions of strategy for the Anglo-American working class.

The Negro question developed as an antithetical element in the growth of the State of the USNA. The bourgeois revolution of 1776 was also a turning point in the development of Negro slavery. Engels wrote:

> ...the American Constitution, the first to recognize the rights of man, in the same breath confirmed the slavery of the colored races in America; class privileges were proscribed, race privileges sanctified.(1)

In a like manner, the development of USNA imperialism—its assuming an international character—was paced with the development of the national character of the Negro question. The keystone of revolution is the resolution of the Negro question, just as this question is the keystone to the introduction of fascism in the United States of North America as a whole.

History has repeatedly proven that any attempt of the Anglo-American working class to move forward and not take full account of the Negro question is doomed to failure. The sorry history of the C.I.O. is proof enough.

We communists of the Communist Labor Party are the most passionate crusaders for justice and morality. We have a sense of moral revulsion and outrage when we daily see the humiliating oppression and ruthless exploitation of the Negro people. Not only because we hate national oppression and national privilege but also because it is that very national oppression of the Negro Nation which fastens ever tighter the chains of capitalist exploitation on the Anglo-American working class.

Leninism defines the political nature of imperialism as reaction down the line. This is doubly true regarding USNA imperialism and triply true in relation to the Negro Nation. All the prayers, pious resolutions and Christian self-sacrifice of life and liberty will not bring independence and democracy one bit closer for the Negro Nation. There are no more reforms left in USNA imperialism. Historically it is transforming into Socialism. The only path is the path of revolution, the path of socialist reconstruction of the United States of North America.

We face a difficult task. The class struggle and social struggle are being waged without a mature Marxist-Leninist Communist Party. It is the very difficult and contradictory nature of the task of building a revolutionary Communist Party that suggests its resolution—that is, to build such a party on the basis of the fact that the Negro question, a national colonial question, is key to the Socialist revolution in the USNA. It is key to the unity of the working class, key to the alliance of the Latin American masses and the Anglo-American proletariat.

The political movements that preceded the Communist Labor Party—from the New York Communist Clubs down to the decrepit revisionist CPUSA—have all been smashed to smithereens on this rock of the Negro question.

We believe that we have fundamentally proven our point on the Negro question. Now we must match the struggle for theoretical clarity with an aggressive practical and revolutionary struggle for the unity of the proletariat.

We call upon those who have read this document and basically agree with it to join us in militantly answering the call of history!

WIN THE PROLETARIAT TO THE CAUSE OF COMMUNISM!

INDEPENDENCE FOR THE NEGRO NATION!

EQUAL RIGHTS FOR THE NEGRO NATIONAL MINORITY!

APPENDIX

Introduction

The following appendix contains the two resolutions on the Negro National question passed by the Communist International in October 1928 and October 1930. Together, these resolutions lay the foundation for any really scientific investigation of the Negro question. The reader will note some obvious and sharp differences between the position of the CLP and the position of the Communist International at that time. Such differences are natural when viewed over a forty year span. This is so, first of all, because the world is in constant flux and the truths of yesteryear are not entirely applicable today. Our knowledge of truth grows dialectically. That is to say that we approach our understanding of reality by constantly taking on new concepts that conform more closely to objective reality and casting aside those concepts that contradict this reality. So it is with the development of the Negro question. Therefore it is with a sense of pride and with a firm knowledge of our historical continuity that we present these valuable historic political documents.

Also included in this appendix are three articles taken from the *People's Tribune,* the political paper of the Communist Labor Party; "Socialism the Only Road", "Are There Races?", and "What are National Minorities?"

Also included are supplementary charts which provide statistics on the economic and social status of Negroes in the USNA.

In addition, we invite the reader to study the pamphlet of the Communist Party, written by Gus Hall in 1952 entitled "Marxism and the Negro Question". Of course, the CPUSA has long ago repudiated that document. However, it is the highest mark of theoretical understanding of the Negro question in the CPUSA. Despite its subjectivity and some gross theoretical errors "Marxism and the Negro Question", along with the resolutions of the Comintern provide the basis for the present work of the Communist Labor Party.

RESOLUTIONS OF THE COMMUNIST INTERNATIONAL ON THE NEGRO QUESTION IN THE UNITED STATES

1. RESOLUTION OF COMMUNIST INTERNATIONAL, OCTOBER, 1930

1. The Communist Party of the United States has always acted openly and energetically against Negro oppression and has thereby won increasing sympathy among the Negro population. In its own ranks, too, the Party has relentlessly fought the slightest evidence of white chauvinism, and has purged itself of the gross opportunism of the Lovestoneites. According to the assertions of these people, the "industrial revolution" will sweep away the remnants of slavery in the agricultural South, and will proletarianize the Negro peasantry, so that the Negro question, as a special national question, would thereby be presumably solved, or could be put off until the time of the socialist revolution in America. But the Party has not yet succeeded in overcoming in its own ranks all underestimation of the struggle for the slogan of the right of self-determination, and still less succeeded in doing away with all *lack of clarity* on the Negro question. In the Party discussion of the question was often wrongly put and much erroneous counterpoising of phrases of the question occurred; thus, for instance: Should the slogan of social equality *or* the slogan of the right of self-determination of the Negroes be emphasized? Should only propaganda for the Negroes' right of self-determination be carried on, or should this slogan be considered as a slogan of action? Should separatist tendencies among the Negroes be supported or opposed? Is the Southern region, thickly populated by Negroes to be looked upon as a colony, or as an "integral part of the national economy of the United States," where presumably a revolutionary situation cannot arise independent of the general revolutionary development in the United States?

In the interest of the utmost clarity of ideas on this question, the Negro question in the United States must be viewed from the standpoint of its peculiarity, namely, as the question of an *oppressed nation,* which is in a peculiar and extraordinarily distressing situation of national oppression not only in view of the prominent *racial distinctions* (marked difference in the color of skin, etc.), but above all, because of considerable *social antagonism* (remnants of slavery). This introduces into the American Negro question an important,

134

peculiar trait which is absent from the national question of other oppressed peoples. Furthermore, it is necessary to face clearly the inevitable distinction between the position of the Negro in the *South* and in the *North,* owing to the fact that at least three-fourths of the entire *Negro* population in the United States (12,000,000) live in compact masses in the South, most of them being peasants and agricultural laborers in a state of semi-serfdom, settled in the "Black Belt" and constituting the majority of the population, whereas the Negroes in the northern states are for the most part industrial workers of the lowest categories who have recently come to the various industrial centers from the South (having often even fled from there).

The struggle of the Communists for the *equal rights* of the Negroes applies to all Negroes, in the North as well as in the South. The struggle for this slogan embraces all or almost all of the important special interests of the Negroes in the North, but not in the South, where the main Communist slogan must be: *The Right of Self-Determination of the Negroes in the Black Belt.* These two slogans, however, are most closely connected. The Negroes in the North are very much interested in winning the right of self-determination of the Negro population of the Black Belt and can thereby hope for strong support for the establishment of true equality of the Negroes in the North. In the South the Negroes are suffering no less, but still more than in the North from the glaring lack of all equality; for the most part the struggle for their most urgent partial demands in the Black Belt is nothing more than the struggle for their equal rights, and only the fulfillment of their main slogan, the right of self-determination in the Black Belt, can assure them of true equality.

THE STRUGGLE FOR THE EQUAL RIGHTS OF THE NEGROES

2. The basis for the demand of equality of the Negroes is provided by the *special* yoke to which the Negroes in the United States are subjected by the ruling classes. In comparison with the situation of the other various nationalities and races oppressed by American imperialism, the yoke of the Negroes in the United States is of a peculiar nature and particularly oppressive. This is partly due to the historical past of the American Negroes as imported slaves, but is

much more due to the still existing slavery of the American Negro which is immediately apparent, for example, in comparing their situation even with the situation of the Chinese and Japanese workers in the West of the United States, or with the lot of the Filipinos (Malay race) who are under colonial repression.

It is only a Yankee bourgeois lie to say that the yoke of Negro slavery has been lifted in the United States. Formally it has been abolished, but in practice the great majority of the Negro masses in the South are living in slavery in the literal sense of the word. Formally, they are "free" as "tenant farmers" or "contract laborers" on the big plantations of the white land owners, but actually they are completely in the power of their exploiters; they are not permitted, or else it is made impossible for them to leave their exploiters; if they do leave the plantations, they are brought back and in many cases whipped; many of them are simply taken prisoner under various pretexts and, bound together with long chains, they have to do compulsory labor on the roads. All through the South, the Negroes are not only deprived of all rights, and subjected to the arbitrary will of the white exploiters, but they are also socially ostracized, that is, they are treated in general not as human beings, but as cattle. But this ostracism regarding Negroes is not limited to the South. Not only in the South but throughout the United States, the lynching of Negroes is permitted to go unpunished. Everywhere the American bourgeoisie surrounds the Negroes with an atmosphere of social ostracism.

The 100 per cent Yankee arrogance divides the American population into a series of castes, among which the Negroes constitute, so to speak, the caste of the "untouchables," who are in a still lower category than the lowest categories of human society, the immigrant laborers, the yellow immigrants, and the Indians. In all big cities the Negroes have to live in special segregated Ghettoes (and of course, have to pay extremely high rent). In practice, marriage between Negroes and whites is prohibited and in the South this is even forbidden by law. In various other ways, the Negroes are segregated, and if they overstep the bounds of the segregation they immediately run the risk of being ill-treated by the 100 per cent bandits. As wage earners, the Negroes are forced to perform the lowest and most difficult work; they generally receive lower wages than the white workers and do not always get the same wages as white workers doing similar work, and their treatment is the very worst. Many

American Federation of Labor Trade unions do not admit Negro workers in their ranks, and a number have organized special trade unions for Negroes so that they will not have to let them into their "good white society."

This whole system of "segregation" and "Jim-Crowism" is special form of national and social oppression under which the American Negroes have much to suffer. The origin of all this is not difficult to find: this Yankee arrogance towards the Negroes stinks of the disgusting atmosphere of the old slave market. This is downright robbery and slave whipping barbarism at the peak of capitalist "culture."

3. The demand for equal rights in our sense of the word, means not only demanding the same rights for the Negroes as the whites have in the United States at the present time, but also demanding that the Negroes should be granted all rights and other advantages which we demand for the corresponding oppressed classes of whites (workers and other toilers). Thus in our sense of the word, the demand for equal rights means a continuous work of abolishment of all forms of economic and political oppression of the Negroes, as well as their social exclusion, the insults perpetrated against them and their segregation. This is to be obtained by constant struggle by the white and black workers for effective legal protection of the Negroes in all fields, as well as actual enforcement of their equality and the combating of every expression of Negrophobia. One of the Communist slogans is: Death for Negro lynching!

The struggle for the equal rights of the Negroes does not in any way exclude recognition and support for the Negroes' right to their own special schools, government organs, etc., wherever the Negro masses put forward such national demands of their own accord. This will, however, in all probability occur to any great extent only in the Black Belt. In other parts of the country the Negroes suffer above all from being shut out from the general social institutions and not from being prohibited from setting up their own national institutions. With the development of the Negro intellectuals (principally in the "free" *professions*) and of a thin layer of small capitalist business people, there have appeared lately not only definite efforts for developing a purely national Negro culture, but also outspoken bourgeois tendencies towards Negro nationalism. The broad masses of the Negro population in the big industrial centers of the North are, however, making no efforts whatsoever to maintain and cultivate a national aloofness. They are, on the contrary, working for assimilation. This effort of the Negro masses can do much in the future to facilitate the progressive process of amalgamating the whites and Negroes into *one* nation, and it is under no circumstances the task of the Communists to give support to bourgeois nationalism in its fight with the progressive assimilation tendencies of the Negro working masses.

4. The slogan of equal rights of the Negroes *without a relentless struggle in practice against all manifestations of Negrophobia on the part of the American bourgeoisie* can be nothing but a deceptive liberal gesture of a sly slave owner or his agent. This slogan is in fact repeated by "socialist" and many other bourgeois politicians and philanthropists, who want to get publicity for themselves by appealing to the "sense of justice" of the American bourgeoisie in the individual treatment of the Negroes, and thereby side-track attention from the one effective struggle against the shameful system of "white superiority": from the *class struggle against the American bourgeoisie.* The struggle for equal rights for the Negroes is, in fact, one of the most important parts of the proletarian class struggle of the United States.

The struggle for equal rights for the Negroes must certainly take the form of common struggle by the white and black workers.

The increasing unity of the various working class elements provokes constant attempts on the part of the American bourgeoisie to play one group against another, particularly the white workers against the black, and the black workers against the immigrant workers, and vice versa, and thus to promote the divisions within the working class, which contribute to the bolstering up of American capitalist rule. The Party must carry on a ruthless struggle against all these attempts of the bourgeoisie and do everything to strengthen the bonds of class solidarity of the working class on a lasting basis.

In the struggle for equal rights for the Negroes, however, it is the duty of the *white* workers to march *at the head* of the struggle. They must everywhere make a breach in the walls of segregation and "Jim-Crowism" which have been set up by bourgeois slave-market morality. They must most ruthlessly unmask and condemn the hypocritical reformists and bourgeois "friends of Negroes" who, in reality, are only interested in strengthening the power of the enemies of the Negroes. They, the white workers, must boldly jump at the throat of the 100 per cent bandits who strike a Negro in the face. This struggle will be the test of real international solidarity of the American white workers.

It is the special duty of the revolutionary Negro workers to carry on tireless activity among the Negro working masses to free them of their distrust of the white proletariat and draw them into the common front of the revolutionary class struggle against the bourgeoisie. They must emphasize with all force that the first rule of proletarian morality is that no worker who wants to be an equal member of *his class* must ever serve as a strike breaker or a supporter of bourgeois politics. They must ruthlessly unmask all Negro politicians corrupted or directly bribed by American bourgeois ideology, who systematically interfere with the real proletarian struggle for equal rights for the Negroes.

Furthermore, the Communist Party must resist all tendencies within its own ranks to ignore the Negro question as a national question in the United States, not only in the South but also in the North. It is advisable for the Communist Party in the North to abstain from the establishment of any special Negro organizations, and in place of this to bring the black and white workers together in common organizations of struggle and joint action. Effective steps must be taken for the organization of Negro workers in the Trade Union Unity League and revolutionary trade unions. Underestimation of this work takes various forms: lack of energy in recruiting Negro workers, in keeping them in our ranks and in drawing them into the full life of the trade unions, selecting, educating and promoting Negro forces to leading functions in the organizations.

The Party must make itself entirely responsible for the carrying through of this very important work. It is most urgently necessary to publish a popular mass paper dealing with the Negro question, edited by white and black comrades, and to have all active followers of this paper grouped organizationally.

II. The Struggle for the Right of Self-Determination of the Negroes in the Black Belt

5. It is not correct to consider the Negro zone of the South as a colony of the United States. Such a characterization of the Black Belt could be based in some respects only upon artificially construed analogies, and would create superfluous difficulties for the

clarification of ideas. In rejecting this estimation, however, it should not be overlooked that it would be none the less false to try to make a fundamental distinction between the character of national oppression to which the colonial peoples are subjected and the yoke of other oppressed nations. Fundamentally, national oppression in both cases is of the same character, and is in the Black Belt in many respects worse than in a number of actual colonies. On one hand the Black Belt is not in itself, either economically or politically, such a united whole as to warrant its being called a special colony of the United States. But on the other hand, this zone is not, either economically or politically, such an integral part of the United States as any other part of the country. Industrialization in the Black Belt is not, as is generally the case in colonies, properly speaking, in contradiction with the ruling interests of the imperialist bourgeoisie, which has in its hands the monopoly of all the industry; but insofar as industry is developed here, it will in no way bring a solution to the question of living conditions of the oppressed Negro majority, nor to the agrarian question, which lies at the basis of the national question. On the contrary, this question is still further aggravated as a result of the increase of the contradictions arising from the pre-capitalist forms of exploitation of the Negro peasantry and of a considerable portion of the Negro proletariat (miners, forestry workers, etc.) in the Black Belt, and at the same time, owing to the industrial development here, the growth of the most important driving force of the national revolution, the black working class, is especially strengthened. Thus, the prospect for the future is not an inevitable dying away of the national revolutionary Negro movement in the South, as Lovestone prophesied, but on the contrary, a great advance of this movement and the rapid approach of a revolutionary crisis in the Black Belt.

6. Owing to the peculiar situation in the Black Belt (the fact that the majority of the resident Negro population are farmers and agricultural laborers and that the capitalist economic system as well as political class rule there is not only of a special kind, but to a great extent still has pre-capitalist and semi-colonial features), the right of self-determination of the Negroes as the *main slogan* of the Communist Party in the Black Belt is appropriate. This, however, does not in any way mean that the struggle for equal rights of the Negroes in the Black Belt is less necessary or less well founded than it is in the North. On the contrary, here, owing to the whole situation,

140

this struggle is even better founded; but the form of this slogan does not sufficiently correspond with the *concrete* requirements of the liberation struggle of the Negro population. Anyway, it is clear that in most cases it is a question of the daily conflicts of interest between the Negroes and the white rulers in the Black Belt on the subject of infringement of the most elementary equality rights of the Negroes by the whites. Daily events of the kind are: all Negro persecutions, all arbitrary economic acts of robbery by the white exploiters ("Black Man's Burden") and the whole system of so-called "Jim- Crowism." Here, however, it is very important in connection with all these concrete cases of conflict to concentrate the attention of the Negro masses not so much on the general demands of mere equality, but much more on some of the revolutionary *basic demands* arising from the concrete situation.

The slogan of the right of self-determination occupies the central place in the liberation struggle of the Negro population in the Black Belt against the yoke of American imperialism. But this slogan, as we see it, must be carried out only in connection with two other basic demands. Thus, there are three basic demands to be kept in mind in the Black Belt, namely, the following:

(a) *Confiscation of the landed property of the white landowners and capitalists for the benefit of the Negro farmers.* The landed property in the hands of the white American exploiters constitutes the most important material basis of the entire system of national oppression and serfdom of the Negroes in the Black Belt. More than three-quarters of all Negro farmers here are bound in actual serfdom to the farms and plantations of the white exploiters by the feudal system of "share cropping." Only on paper and not in practice are they freed from the yoke of their former slavery. The same holds completely true for the great mass of black contract laborers. Here the contract is only the capitalist expression of the chains of the old slavery, which even today are not infrequently applied in their natural iron form on the roads of the Black Belt (chain gang work). These are the main forms of present Negro slavery in the Black Belt, and no breaking of the chains of this slavery is possible without confiscating all the landed property of the white masters. Without this revolutionary measure, without the agrarian revolution, the right of self-determination of the Negro population would be only a Utopia or, at best, would remain only on paper without changing in any way the actual enslavement.

(b) *Establishment of the state unity of the Black Belt.* At the present time this Negro zone—precisely for the purpose of facilitating national oppression—is artificially split up and divided into a number of various states which include distant localities having a majority of white population. If the right of self-determination of the Negroes is to be put into force, it is necessary wherever possible to bring together into one governmental unit all districts of the South where the majority of the settled population consists of Negroes. Within the limits of this state there will of course remain a fairly significant white minority which must submit to the right of self-determination of the Negro majority. There is no other possible way of carrying out in a democratic manner the right of self-determination of the Negroes. Every plan regarding the establishment of the Negro state with an exclusively Negro population in America (and of course, still more exporting it to Africa) is nothing but an unreal and reactionary caricature of the fulfillment of the right of self-determination of the Negroes, and every attempt to isolate and transport the Negroes would have the most damaging effect upon their interests. Above all, it would violate the right of the Negro farmers in the Black Belt not only to their present residences and their land, but also to the land owned by the white landlords and cultivated by Negro labor.

(c) *Right of self-determination.* This means complete and unlimited right of the Negro majority to exercise governmental authority in the entire territory of the Black Belt, as well as to decide upon the relations between their territory and other nations, particularly the United States. It would not be right of self-determination in our sense of the word if the Negroes in the Black Belt had the right of self-determination only in cases which concerned *exclusively* the Negroes and did not affect the whites, because the most important cases arising here are bound to affect the whites as well as Negroes. First of all, true right to self-determination means that the Negro majority and not the white minority in the entire territory of the administratively united Black Belt exercises the right of administering governmental, legislative, and judicial authority. At the present time all this power is concentrated in the hands of the white bourgeoisie and landlords. It is they who appoint all officials, it is they who dispose of public property, it is they who determine the taxes, it is they who govern and make the laws. Therefore, *the overthrow of this class rule* in the Black Belt is unconditionally necessary in the struggle for the Negroes' right to self-determination. This, however, means at the same time the overthrow of the yoke of American imperialism in the Black Belt on which the forces of the local white bourgeoisie depend. Only in this way, only if the Negro population of the Black Belt wins its freedom from American imperialism even to the point of deciding *itself* the relations between its country and other governments, especially the United States, will it win real and complete self-determination. One should demand from the beginning that no armed forces of American imperialism should remain on the territory of the Black Belt.

As stated in the letter of the Political Secretariat of the E.C.C.I. of March 16, 1930, the Communists must "*unreservedly* carry on a struggle" for the self-determination of the Negro population in the Black Belt in accordance with what has been set forth above. It is incorrect and harmful to interpret the Communist stand point to mean that the Communists stand for the right of self-determination of the Negroes only up to a certain point but not beyond this, to, for example, the right of separation. It is also incorrect to say that the Communists are only to carry on propaganda or agitation for the right of self-determination, but not to develop any activity to bring this about. No, it is of the utmost importance for the Communist Party to reject any such limitation of its struggle for this slogan. Even if the situation does not yet warrant the raising of the question of uprising, one should not limit oneself at present to propaganda for the demand, "Right of Self-Determination," but should organize mass actions, such as demonstrations, strikes, tax boycott movements, etc.

Moreover, the Party cannot make its stand for this slogan dependent upon any conditions, even the condition that the proletariat has the hegemony in the national revolutionary Negro movement or that the majority of the Negro population in the Black Belt adopts the Soviet form (as Pepper demanded), etc. It goes without saying that the Communists in the Black Belt will and must try to win over all working elements of the Negroes, that is, the majority of the population, to their side and to convince them not only that they must win the right of self-determination but also that they must make use of this right in accordance with the Communist program. But this cannot be made a *condition* for the stand of the Communists in favor of the right of self-determination of the Negro population. If, or so long as, the majority of this population wishes to handle the situation in the Black Belt in a different manner from that which we Communists would like, its complete right to self-determination must be recognized. This right we must defend as a free democratic right.

8. In general, the Communist Party of the United States has kept to this correct line recently in its struggle for the right of self-determination of the Negroes, even though this line—in some cases— has been unclearly or erroneously expressed. In particular, some misunderstanding has arisen from the failure to make a clear distinction between the demand for "right of self-determination" and the demand for governmental separation, simply treating these two demands in the same way. However, these two demands are not identical. Complete right to self-determination includes also the right to governmental separation, but does not necessarily imply that the Negro population should *make use of this* right in all circumstances, that is, that it must actually separate or attempt to separate the Black Belt from the existing governmental federation with the United States. If it desires to separate, it must be free to do so; but if it prefers to remain federated with the United States it must also be free to do that. This is the correct meaning of the idea of self-determination, and it must be recognized quite independently of whether the United States is still a capitalist state or whether a proletarian dictatorship has already been established there.

It is, however, another matter if it is not a case of the *right* of the oppressed nation concerned to separate or to maintain governmental contact, but if the question is treated on its merits: whether it is to work for state separation, whether it is to struggle *for this* or not. This is another question, on which the stand of the Communists must *vary* according to the concrete conditions. If the proletariat has come into power in the United States, the Communist Negroes will not come out for but *against* separation of the Negro Republic from federation with the United States. But the *right* of the Negroes to governmental separation will be *unconditionally realized* by the Communist Party; it will unconditionally give the Negro population of the Black Belt freedom of choice even on this question. Only when the proletariat has come into power in the United States the Communists will carry on propaganda among the working masses of the Negro population against separation, in order to convince them that it is much better and in the interest of the Negro nation for the Black Belt to be a free republic, where the Negro majority has complete right of self-determination but remains governmentally federated with the great proletarian republic of the United States. The bourgeois counter-revolutionists, on the other hand, will then be interested in boosting the separation tendencies in the ranks of the various nationalities in order to utilize separatist nationalism as a barrier for the bourgeois counter-revolution against the consolidation of the proletarian dictatorship.

But the question at the present time is not this. As long as capitalism rules in the United States the Communists cannot come out against governmental separation of the Negro zone from the United States. They recognize that this separation from the imperialist United States would be preferable, from the standpoint of the national interests of the Negro population, to their present oppressed state, and therefore, the Communists are ready at any time to offer all their support if only the working masses of the Negro population are ready to take up the struggle for governmental independence of the Black Belt. At the present time, however, the situation in the national struggle in the South is not such as to win mass support of the working Negroes for this separatist struggle; and it is not the task of Communists to call upon them to separate, without taking into consideration the existing situation and the desires of the Negro masses.

The situation in the Negro question in the United States, however, may undergo a radical change. It is even probable that the separatist efforts to obtain complete state independence of the Black Belt will gain ground among the Negro masses of the South in the near future. This is connected with the prospective sharpening of the national conflicts in the South, with the advance of the national revolutionary Negro movement, and with the exceptionally brutal fascist aggressiveness of the white exploiters of the South, as well as with the support of this aggressiveness by the central government authority of the United States. In this sharpening of the situation in the South, Negro separatism will presumably increase, and the question of independence of the Black Belt will become the question of the day. Then the Communist Party must also face this question and, if the circumstances seem favorable, must stand up with all strength and courage for the struggle to win independence and for the establishment of a Negro republic in the Black Belt.

9. The general relation of Communists to separatist tendencies among the Negroes, described above, cannot mean that Communists

associate themselves at present, or generally speaking, during capitalism, indiscriminately and without criticism with all the separatist currents of the various bourgeois or petty bourgeois Negro groups. For there is not only a national-revolutionary, but also a reactionary Negro separatism, for instance, that represented by Garvey. His Utopia of an isolated Negro state (regardless of whether in Africa or America, if it is supposed to consist of Negroes only) pursues only the political aim of diverting the Negro masses from the real liberation struggle against American imperialism.

It would be a mistake to imagine that the "right of self-determination" slogan is a truly revolutionary slogan only in connection with the demand for complete separation. *The question of power is decided not only through* the demand of separation, but just as much through the demand of the *right* to decide the separation question and self-determination in general. A direct question of power is also the demand of confiscation of the land of the white exploiters in the South, as well as the demand of the Negroes that the entire Black Belt be amalgamated into a state unit.

Hereby, every single fundamental demand of the liberation struggle of the Negroes in the Black Belt is such that—if once thoroughly understood by the Negro masses and adopted as their slogan—it will lead them into the struggle for the overthrow of the power of the ruling bourgeoisie, which is impossible without such revolutionary struggle. One cannot deny that it is just possible for the Negro population of the Black Belt to win the right to self-determination during capitalism; but it is perfectly clear and indubitable that this is possible only through successful revolutionary struggle for power against the American bourgeoisie, through *wresting* the Negroes' right of self-determination from American imperialism. Thus, the slogan of right to self-determination is a real slogan of national rebellion which, to be considered as such, need not be supplemented by proclaiming struggle for the complete separation of the Negro zone, at least not at present. But it must be made perfectly clear to the Negro masses that the slogan "Right to self-determination" includes the demand of full freedom for them to decide even the question of complete separation. We demand freedom of separation, real right of self-determination, wrote Lenin, "certainly not in order to 'recommend' separation, but on the contrary, in order to facilitate and accelerate the democratic rapprochement and unification of nations." For the same purpose, Lenin's party, the

Communist Party of the Soviet Union, bestowed after its seizure of power on all the peoples hitherto oppressed by Russian Tsarism, the full right to self-determination, including the right of complete separation, and achieved thereby its enormous successes with regard to the democratic rapprochement and voluntary unification of nations.

10. The slogan for the right of self-determination and the other fundamental slogans of the Negro question in the Black Belt do not exclude but rather pre-suppose an energetic development of the struggle for concrete *partial demands* linked up with the daily needs and afflictions of wide masses of working Negroes. In order to avoid, in this connection, the danger of opportunist back-slidings, Communists must above all remember this:

(a) The direct aims and partial demands around which a partial struggle develops are to be linked up in the course of the struggle with the revolutionary fundamental slogans brought up by the question of power, in a popular manner corresponding to the mood of the masses. (Confiscation of the big landholdings, establishment of governmental unity of the Black Belt, right of self-determination of the Negro population in the Black Belt.) Bourgeois-socialist tendencies to oppose such a revolutionary widening and deepening of the fighting demands must be fought.

(b) One should not venture to draw up a complete program of some kind, or a system of "positive" partial demands. Such programs on the part of petty-bourgeois politicians should be exposed as attempts to divert the masses from the necessary hard struggles by fostering reformist and democratic illusions among them. Every positive partial demand which might crop up is to be considered from the viewpoint of whether it is in keeping with our revolutionary fundamental slogans or whether it is of a reformist or reactionary tendency. Every kind of national oppression which arouses the indignation of the Negro masses can be used as a suitable point of departure for the development of partial struggles, during which the abolition of such oppressions, as well as their prevention through revolutionary struggle against the ruling exploiting dictatorship, must be demanded.

(c) Everything should be done to bring wide masses of Negroes into these partial struggles. This is important—and not to carry the various partial demands to such an ultra-radical point that the mass of working Negroes are no longer able to recognize them as *their own.* Without a real mobilization of the mass-movements—in spite of the sabotage of the bourgeois reformist Negro politicians—even the best Communist partial demands get hung up. On the other hand, even some relatively insignificant acts of the Ku Klux Klan bandits in the Black Belt can become the occasion of important political movements, provided the Communists are able to organize the resistance of the indignant Negro masses. In such cases, mass movements of this kind can easily develop into real rebellion. This rests on the fact that—as Lenin said—"Every act of national oppression calls forth resistance on the part of the masses of the population, and the tendency of every act of resistance on the part of oppressed peoples is the national uprising."

(d) Communists must fight in the *forefront* of the national-liberation movement and must do their utmost for the progress of this mass movement and its revolutionization. Negro Communists must *clearly dissociate* themselves from all bourgeois currents in the Negro movement, must indefatigably oppose the spread of the influence of the bourgeois groups on the working Negroes. In dealing with them they must apply the Communist tactic laid down by the Sixth C.I. Congress with regard to the colonial question, in order to guarantee *the hegemony of the Negro proletariat* in the national liberation movement of the Negro population and to coordinate wide masses of the Negro peasantry in a steady fighting alliance with the proletariat.

(e) One must work with the utmost energy for the establishment and consolidation of *Communist Party organizations* and revolutionary *trade unions* in the South. Furthermore, immediate measures must be taken for the organization of proletarian and peasant *self-defense* against the Ku Klux Klan. For this purpose the Communist Party is to give further instructions.

11. It is particularly incumbent on Negro Communists to criticize consistently the half-heartedness and hesitations of the petty-bourgeois national-revolutionary Negro leaders in the liberation struggle of the Black Belt, exposing them before the masses. All national reformist currents as, for instance, Garveyism, which are an obstacle to the revolutionization of the Negro masses, must be fought systematically and with the utmost energy. Simultaneously, Negro Communists must carry on among the Negro masses an energetic struggle against nationalist moods directed indiscriminately against all whites, workers as well as capitalists, Communists as well as imperialists. Their constant call to the Negro masses must

be: *Revolutionary struggle against the ruling white bourgeoisie, through a fighting alliance with the revolutionary white proletariat!* Negro Communists must indefatigably explain to the mass of the Negro population that even if many white workers in America are still infected with Negrophobia, the American proletariat, as a class, which owing to its struggle against the American bourgeoisie represents the only truly revolutionary class, will be the only real mainstay of Negro liberation. Insofar as successes in the national-revolutionary struggle of the Negro population of the South for its right to self-determination are already possible under capitalism, they can be achieved only if this struggle is effectively supported by proletarian mass actions on a large scale in the other parts of the United States. But it is also clear that "only a victorious proletarian revolution will *finally decide* the agrarian question and the national question in the South of the United States, in the interest of the predominating mass of the Negro population of the country." (*Colonial Theses of the Sixth World Congress.*)

12. The struggle regarding the Negro question in the North must be linked up with the liberation struggle in the South, in order to endow the Negro movement throughout the United States with the necessary effective strength. After all, in the North, as well as in the South, it is a question of the real emancipation of the American Negroes, which has in fact never taken place. The Communist Party of the United States must bring into play its entire revolutionary energy, in order to mobilize the widest possible masses of the white and black proletariat of the United States, not by words, but by deeds, for real effective support of the struggle for the liberation of the Negroes. Enslavement of the Negroes is one of the most important foundations of the imperialist dictatorship of United States capitalism. The more American imperialism fastens its yoke on the millions-strong Negro masses, the more must the Communist Party develop the mass struggle for Negro emancipation, and the better use it must make of all conflicts which arise out of the national difference, as an incentive for revolutionary mass actions against the bourgeoisie. This is as much in the direct interest of the proletarian revolution in America. Whether the rebellion of the Negroes is to be the outcome of a general revolutionary situation in the United States, whether it is to originate in the whirlpool of decisive fights for power by the working class, for proletarian dictatorship, or whether on the contrary the Negro rebellion will be the prelude of

gigantic struggles for power by the American proletariat, cannot be foretold now. But in either contingency it is essential for the Communist Party *to make an energetic beginning now—at the present moment—with the organization of joint mass struggles* of white and black workers against Negro oppression. This alone will enable us to get rid of the bourgeois white chauvinism which is polluting the ranks of the white workers in America, to overcome the distrust of the Negro masses caused by the inhumane barbarous Negro slave traffic still carried on by the American bourgeoisie—inasmuch as it is directed even against all white workers—and to win over to our side these millions of Negroes as active fellow-fighters in the struggle for the overthrow of bourgeois power throughout America.

2. RESOLUTION OF COMMUNIST INTERNATIONAL, OCTOBER 26, 1928

1. The industrialization of the South, the concentration of a new Negro working class population in the big cities of the East and North and the entrance of the Negroes into the basic industries on a mass scale, create the possibility for the Negro workers, under the leadership of the Communist Party, to assume the hegemony of all Negro liberation movements, and to increase their importance and role in the revolutionary struggle of the American proletariat.

The Negro working class has reached a stage of development which enables it, if properly organized and well led, to fulfill successfully its double historical mission: (a) to play a considerable role in the class struggle against American imperialism as an important part of the American working class; and (b) to lead the movement of the oppressed masses of the Negro population.

2. The bulk of the Negro population (86 per cent) live in the southern states; of this number 74 per cent live in the rural districts and are dependent almost exclusively upon agriculture for a livelihood. Approximately one-half of these rural dwellers live in the so-called "Black Belt," in which area they constitute more than 50 per cent of the entire population. The great mass of the Negro agrarian population are subject to the most ruthless exploitation and persecution of a semi-slave character. In addition to the ordinary forms of capitalist exploitation, American imperialism utilizes every possible form of slave exploitation (peonage, share-cropping, landlord supervision of crops and marketing, etc.) for the purpose of extracting

super-profits. On the basis of these slave remnants, there has grown up a super-structure of social and political inequality that expresses itself in lynching, segregation, Jim-Crowism, etc.

Necessary Conditions for National Revolutionary Movement

3. The various forms of oppression of the Negro masses, who are concentrated mainly in the so-called "Black Belt," provide the necessary conditions for a national revolutionary movement among the Negroes. The Negro agricultural laborers and the tenant farmers feel the pressure of white persecution and exploitation. Thus, the agrarian problem lies at the root of the Negro national movement. The great majority of Negroes in the rural districts of the South are not "reserves of capitalist reaction," but potential allies of the revolutionary proletariat. Their objective position facilitates their transformation into a revolutionary force, which, under the leadership of the proletariat, will be able to participate in the joint struggle with all other workers against capitalist exploitation.

4. It is the duty of the Negro workers to organize through the mobilization of the broad masses of the Negro population the struggle of the agricultural laborers and tenant farmers against all forms of semi-feudal oppression. On the other hand, it is the duty of the Communist Party of the U.S.A. to mobilize and rally the broad masses of the white workers for active participation in this struggle. For that reason the Party must consider the beginning of systematic work in the South as one of its main tasks, having regard for the fact that the bringing together of the workers and toiling masses of all nationalities for a joint struggle against the land-owners and the bourgeoisie is one of the most important aims of the Communist International, as laid down in the resolutions on the national and colonial question of the Second and Sixth Congresses of the Comintern.

For Complete Emancipation of Oppressed Negro Race

5. To accomplish this task, the Communist Party must come out as the champion of the right of the oppressed Negro race for full emancipation. While continuing and intensifying the struggle under the slogan of full social and political equality for the Negroes, which must remain the central slogan of our Party for work among

the masses, the Party must come out openly and unreservedly for the right of Negroes to national self-determination in the southern states, where the Negroes form a majority of the population. The struggle for equal rights and the propaganda for the slogan of self-determination must be linked up with the economic demands of the Negro masses, especially those directed against the slave remnants and all forms of national and racial oppression. Special stress must be laid upon organizing active resistance against lynching, Jim-Crowism, segregation and all other forms of oppression of the Negro population.

6. All work among the Negroes, as well as the struggle for the Negro cause among the whites, must be used, based upon the changes which have taken place in the relationship of classes among the Negro population. The existence of a Negro industrial proletariat of almost two million workers makes it imperative that the main emphasis should be placed on these new proletarian forces. The Negro workers must be organized under the leadership of the Communist Party, and thrown into joint struggle together with the white workers. The Party must learn to combine all demands of the Negroes with the economic and political struggle of the workers and the poor farmers.

American Negro Question Part of World Problem

7. The Negro question in the United States must be treated in its relation to the Negro questions and struggles in other parts of the world. The Negro race everywhere is an oppressed race. Whether it is a minority (U.S.A., etc.), majority (South Africa) or inhabits a so-called independent state (Liberia, etc.), the Negroes are oppressed by imperialism. Thus, a common tie of interest is established for the revolutionary struggle of race and national liberation from imperialist domination of the Negroes in various parts of the world. A strong Negro revolutionary movement in the U.S.A. will be able to influence and direct the revolutionary movement in all those parts of the world where the Negroes are oppressed by imperialism.

8. The proletarianization of the Negro masses makes the trade unions the principal form of mass organization. It is the primary task of the Party to play an active part and lead in the work of organizing the Negro workers and agricultural laborers in trade unions. Owing to the refusal of the majority of the white unions in the

U.S.A., led by the reactionary leaders, to admit Negroes to membership, steps must be immediately taken to set up special unions for those Negro workers who are not allowed to join the white unions. At the same time, however, the struggles for the inclusion of Negro workers in the existing unions must be intensified and concentrated upon, special attention must be given to those unions in which the statutes and rules set up special limitations against the admission of Negro workers. The primary duty of the Communist Party in this connection is to wage a merciless struggle against the A.F. of L. bureaucracy, which prevents the Negro workers from joining the white workers' unions. The organization of special trade unions for the Negro masses must be carried out as part and parcel of the struggle against the restrictions imposed upon the Negro workers, and for their admission to the white workers' unions. The creation of separate Negro unions should in no way weaken the struggle in the old unions for the admission of Negroes on equal terms. Every effort must be made to see that all the new unions organized by the left wing and the Communist Party should embrace the workers of all nationalities and of all races. The principle of one union for all workers in each industry, white and black, should cease to be a mere slogan of propaganda, and must become a slogan of action.

Party Trade Union Work Among Negroes

9. While organizing the Negroes into unions and conducting an aggressive struggle against the anti-Negro trade union policy of the A.F. of L., the Party must pay more attention than it has hitherto done to the work in the Negro workers' organizations, such as the Brotherhood of Sleeping Car Porters, Chicago Asphalt Workers Union, and so on. The existence of two million Negro workers and the further industrialization of the Negroes demand a radical change in the work of the Party among the Negroes. The creation of working class organizations and the extension of our influence in the existing working-class Negro organizations, are of much greater importance than the work in bourgeois and petty-bourgeois organizations, such as the National Association for the Advancement of Colored People, the Pan-African Congress, etc.

10. The American Negro Labor Congress continues to exist only nominally. Every effort should be made to strengthen this organization as a medium through which we can extend the work of the

Party among the Negro masses and mobilize the Negro workers under our leadership.

11. The importance of trade union work imposes special tasks upon the Trade Union Unity League. The T.U.U.L. has completely neglected the work among the Negro workers, notwithstanding the fact that these workers are objectively in a position to play a very great part in carrying through the program of organizing the unorganized. The closest contact must be established between the T.U.U.L. and the Negro masses. The T.U.U.L. must become the champion in the struggle for the rights of the Negroes in the old unions, and in the organizing of new unions for both Negroes and whites, as well in separate Negro unions.

White Chauvinism Evidenced in the American Party

12. The C.E.C. of the American Communist Party itself stated in its resolution of April 30, 1928, that "the Party as a whole has not sufficiently realized the significance of work among the Negroes." Such an attitude toward the Party work among the Negroes is, however, not satisfactory. The time is ripe to begin within the Party a courageous campaign of self-criticism concerning the work among the Negroes. Penetrating self-criticism is the necessary preliminary condition for directing the Negro work along new lines.

13. The Party must bear in mind that white chauvinism, which is the expression of the ideological influence of American imperialism among the workers, not only prevails among the different strata of the white workers in the U.S.A., but is even reflected in various forms in the Party itself. White chauvinism has manifested itself even in open antagonism of some comrades to the Negro comrades. In some instances where Communists were called upon to champion and lead in the most vigorous manner the fight against white chauvinism, they instead yielded to it. In Gary, white members of the Workers Party protested against Negroes eating in the restaurant controlled by the Party. In Detroit, Party members, yielding to pressure, drove the Negro comrades from a social given in aid of the miners' strike.

While the Party has taken certain measures against these manifestations of white chauvinism, nevertheless those manifestations must be regarded as indications of race prejudice even in the ranks of the Party, which must be fought with the utmost energy.

154

14. An aggressive fight against all forms of white chauvinism must be accompanied by a widespread and thorough educational campaign in the spirit of internationalism within the Party, utilizing for this purpose to the fullest possible extent the Party schools, the Party press and the public platform, to stamp out all forms of antagonism, or even indifference among our white comrades toward the Negro work. This educational work should be conducted simultaneously with a campaign to draw the white workers and the poor farmers into the struggle for the support of the demands of the Negro workers.

Tasks of the Party in Relation To Negro Work

15. The Communist Party of the U.S.A., in its treatment of the Negro question must all the time bear in mind this twofold task:

(a) To fight for the full rights of the oppressed Negroes and for their right to self-determination and against all forms of chauvinism, especially among the workers of the oppressing nationality.

(b) The propaganda and the day-to-day practice of international class solidarity must be considered as one of the basic tasks of the American Communist Party. The fight—by propaganda and by deeds—should be directed first and foremost against the chauvinism of the workers of the oppressing nationality as well as against bourgeois segregation tendencies of the oppressed nationality. The propaganda of international class solidarity is the necessary prerequisite for the unity of the working class in the struggle.

"The center of gravity in educating the workers of the oppressing countries in the principles of internationalism must inevitably consist in the propaganda and defense of the workers of the right of separation by the oppressed countries. We have the right and duty to treat every socialist of an oppressing nation, who does not conduct such propaganda, as an imperialist and as a scoundrel."

(Lenin, from selected articles on the national question.)

16. The Party must seriously take up the task of training a cadre of Negro comrades as leaders, bring them into the Party schools in the U.S.A. and abroad, and make every effort to draw Negro proletarians into active and leading work in the Party, not confining the activities of the Negro comrades exclusively to the work among

155

Negroes. Simultaneously, white workers must specially be trained for work among the Negroes.

17. Efforts must be made to transform the *Negro Champion* into a weekly mass organ of the Negro proletariat and tenant farmers. Every encouragement and inducement must be given to the Negro comrades to utilize the Party press generally.

Negro Work Part of General Work of the Party

18. The Party must link up the struggle on behalf of the Negroes with the general campaigns of the Party. The Negro problem must be part and parcel of all and every campaign conducted by the Party. In the election campaign, trade union work, the campaigns for the organization of the unorganized, anti-imperialist work, labor party campaign, International Labor Defense, etc., the Central Executive Committee must work out plans designed to draw the Negroes into active participation in all these campaigns, and at the same time to bring the white workers into the struggle on behalf of the Negroes' demands. It must be borne in mind that the Negro masses will not be won for the revolutionary struggles until such time as the most conscious section of the white workers show, by action, that they are fighting with the Negroes against all racial discrimination and persecution. Every member of the Party must bear in mind that "age- long oppression of the colonial and weak nationalities by the imperialist powers, has given rise to a feeling of bitterness among the masses of the enslaved countries as well as a feeling of distrust toward the oppressing nations in general and toward the proletariat of those nations." (See Resolution on Colonial and National Question of Second Congress.)

19. The Negro women in industry and on the farms constitute a powerful potential force in the struggle for Negro emancipation. By reason of being unorganized to an even greater extent than male Negro workers, they are the most exploited section. The A.F. of L. bureaucracy naturally exercises toward them a double hostility, by reason of both their color and sex. It therefore becomes an important task of the Party to bring the Negro women into the economic and political struggle.

20. Only by an active and strenuous fight on the part of the white workers against all forms of oppression directed against the Negroes, will the Party be able to draw into its ranks the most active

and conscious Negro workers—men and women—and to increase its influence in those intermediary organizations which are necessary for the mobilization of the Negro masses in the struggle against segregation, lynching, Jim-Crowism, etc.

21. In the present struggle in the mining industry, the Negro workers participate actively and in large numbers. The leading role the Party played in this struggle has helped greatly to increase its prestige. Nevertheless, the special efforts being made by the Party in the work among the Negro strikers cannot be considered as adequate. The Party did not send enough Negro organizers into the coal fields, and it did not sufficiently attempt, in the first stages of the fight, to develop the most able Negro strikers and to place them in leading positions. The Party must be especially criticized for its failure to put Negro workers on the Presidium of the Pittsburgh Miners' Conference, doing so only after such representation was demanded by the Negroes themselves.

22. In the work among the Negroes, special attention should be paid to the role played by the churches and preachers who are acting on behalf of American imperialism. The Party must conduct a continuous and carefully worked out campaign among the Negro masses, sharpened primarily against the preachers and the churchmen, who are the agents of the oppressors of the Negro race.

Party Work Among Negro Proletariat and Peasantry

23. The Party must apply united front tactics for specific demands to the existing Negro petty bourgeois organizations. The purpose of these united front tactics should be the mobilizing of the Negro masses under the leadership of the Party, and to expose the treacherous petty bourgeois leadership of those organizations.

24. The Negro Miners Relief Committee and the Harlem Tenants League are examples of joint organizations of action which may serve as a means of drawing the Negro masses into struggle. In every case the utmost effort must be made to combine the struggle of the Negro workers with the struggle of the white workers, and to draw the white workers' organizations into such joint campaigns.

25. In order to reach the bulk of the Negro masses, special attention should be paid to the work among the Negroes in the South. For that purpose, the Party should establish a district organization in the most suitable locality in the South. Whilst continuing trade un-

ion work among the Negro workers and the agricultural laborers, special organizations of tenant farmers must be set up. Special efforts must also be made to secure the support of the share croppers in the creation of such organizations. The Party must undertake the task of working out a definite program of immediate demands, directed against all slave remnants, which will serve as the rallying slogans for the formation of such peasant organizations.

Henceforth the Communist Party must consider the struggle on behalf of the Negro masses, the task of organizing the Negro workers and peasants and the drawing of these oppressed masses into the proletarian revolutionary struggle, as one of its major tasks, remembering, in the words of the Second Congress resolution, that "the victory over capitalism cannot be fully achieved and carried to its ultimate goal unless the proletariat and the toiling masses of all nations of the world rally of their own accord in a concordant and close union."

Leninism and Self-Determination

Formerly, the principle of self-determination of nations was wrongly interpreted, and not infrequently it was narrowed down to the right of nations to autonomy. Certain leaders of the Second International went so far as to convert the right of self-determination into a right to cultural autonomy, *i.e.,* they would accord to the oppressed nation the right to have its own cultural institutions while the dominant nation would retain all political power in its own hands. The result was that the idea of self-determination was in danger of becoming a means for justifying annexations rather than a means of fighting against annexations. This confusion has now been cleared up. Leninism has broadened the conception of self-determination, and interprets it as the right of the oppressed peoples in dependent countries and colonies to complete separation, as the right of nations to independent existence as states. This has precluded the possibility of annexations being justified on the grounds that the right of self-determination merely means the right to autonomy. The very principle of self-determination was thus changed from a means to deceive the masses, that it undoubtedly was in the hands of the social-chauvinists during the imperialist war, into an instrument for exposing all imperialist designs or chauvinist machinations, a means of political education of the masses in the spirit of internationalism.

Formerly, the question of the oppressed nations used to be regarded purely as a question of law. Solemn proclamations of "national equality under the law" and innumerable declarations about the "equality of nations" were common stock-in-trade of the parties of the Second International, which served to gloss over the sheer mockery of talking about the "equality of nations" under imperialism while one group of nations (a minority) lives upon the backs of another group of nations whom they exploit. This bourgeois legalistic point of view on the national question has now been completely exposed. Leninism brought the national question down from the lofty heights of high-sounding declarations to the solid ground of facts and declared that pronouncements about the "equality of nations" which are not reinforced by the direct support of the proletarian parties to the liberation movement of the oppressed nations are meaningless and false. In this way the question of the oppressed nations became a question of rendering support and assistance, real and continuous, to the oppressed nations in their struggle against imperialism, their struggle for real equality of nations and for their independent existence as states.—J. Stalin, from *Foundations of Leninism.*

SOCIALISM: THE ONLY ROAD

(from *The People's Tribune,* Vol. 2, No. 3, February 1, 1975)

Negro History Week, 1975, comes at a period of history that demands the most critical examination of the position of the Negro People's National Liberation Movement.

Negro History Week was proclaimed by the government in order to counteract and divert the powerful and growing national liberation movement of the Negro people in the 1940's. Not only did Negro History Week take the place of the militant holidays of June 19th (when slavery was outlawed in the territories) and January 1st (Emancipation Proclamation Day), but close behind this, the stirring Negro national anthem was retitled "Lift Every Voice and Sing" and carefully shelved. Every manifestation in culture and politics of the national character of the Negro people was slowly and carefully isolated and liquidated.

Crucial in this motion was the role of the CPUSA. The Party by 1949 was in utter rout. The leaders—jailed, scared-off or bribed were ready for whatever compromise the government demanded. The disbanding of the Party in the South in 1949, in violation of democratic centralism and the Party program, set the objective political situation for the liquidation of the Marxist line on the Negro Question. The chauvinistic lame duck leadership of the Party did not dare use any of their Anglo-American so-called theoreticians for the task of undoing Lenin's and Stalin's analysis of the Negro Question. However, there has never been a period in history when satraps and sycophants aren't available to do the work that is beneath the intellectual dignity of honorable men and women. Dr. James Jackson, clutching the mantle of "theoretician" that had been bestowed on him by the equally illustrious "theoretician" Gus Hall, stepped up to give a coward's *coup de grace* to an already mortally wounded Marxist policy.

Dr. Jackson's *New Theoretical Aspects on the Negro Question* was added to the long string of "firsts" that he was so prone to boast about: first Negro Eagle Scout in South Carolina, first Negro Ph.D. in South Carolina, and then the first Negro theoretical sycophant in the CPUSA. Standing on the respect that Comrade Pettis Perry had won for the proletarian Negro theoretician, Jackson, backed to the bloody hilt by Gus Hall, Gene Dennis, Foster, Davis, et. al., forced

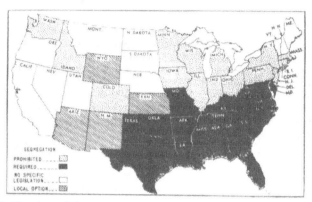

An indication of the status of interracial education in the United States at the time of the Supreme Court decision.

Source: Langston Hughes & Milton Meltzer, A Pictorial History of the Negro in America (New York: Crown Publishers, Inc., 1956)

A map showing the reaction of the various Southern states to the edict on integration a year after the Supreme Court decision.

his rotten document on the Party membership. This document basically stated that the great migrations from the South during the 1940's had resulted in a dispersal of the Negro people and consequently the Negro Nation had ceased to exist.

This position was challenged theoretically by many comrades, but the fact that the dispersal of nations is an inevitable result of imperialist oppression was put aside. The fact that there was not a decline in the absolute number of Negroes in the Black Belt was disregarded. Jackson and the leadership of the Party were presented with facts of the migrations from Ireland and Puerto Rico and the fact that these nations still exist, but these facts were also waived aside. In short, the CPUSA by first abandoning the Marxist position on the national question and then embracing cultural nationalism, created an unprecedented political vacuum in both the Negro People's National Liberation Movement and in the working class.

Under these conditions the theoretical and ideological leadership of the Negro People's National Liberation Movement slipped from the hands of the Negro workers and radical petty bourgeoisie (that were in or influenced by the "Party of the Negro People," the Communist Party) and into the hands of the Negro petty bourgeoisie that was hostile to the working class and communism.

The contradictory, but twin ideologies of the Negro bourgeoisie—integration and black nationalism—were supported all the way by the now discredited CPUSA. It appeared as if reaction was at last victorious and the shattered movement defeated. But life asserts itself and in August, 1965, in Watts, California, the national aspects of the Negro Question were asserted with such violence that every political group in the country was compelled to reassess its position. Today life itself has placed such a searchlight on this question that every progressive group in the country is compelled to at least pay lip service to the partisan, scientific brilliance of Marxism on the National and Colonial Question. We assert today, as we always have, that the Negro Question is the question presented by a historically evolved stable community of people, formed on the basis of a common language, territory, economic life and psychological make-up manifested in a common culture. In the Negro Nation, a colonial nation, every class, with the exception of the comprador bourgeoisie, is oppressed and exploited through the imperialist relations. In a word, the Negro People, oppressed as a nation—socially, politically, and economically shackled by imperialism—cannot free themselves without the overthrow of imperialism. This cannot be accomplished without the abolition of capitalism. This is the only scientific position. It is the position of Marxism.

During the heyday of the "movement" the agents of the bourgeoisie, the so-called leaders, were quick to point to the so-called gains by the Negro masses. To point to such gains means to first describe the journey from where to where. If we were to start at the beginning of this century, we would have to say that the position of the Negro people in 1900 was almost as it had been under slavery Disenfranchised, terrorized by pogroms that rivaled the Black Hundreds in terror and brutality, economically at the very bottom of the ladder, the Negro masses slowly gained consciousness of their collective plight. In a period of identity of interest, the rising Negro national bourgeoisie, peasantry and proletariat began a struggle for equality. This was spelled out as a fight for seniority on the job, for an anti-lynch law, for a voting rights act and for a comprehensive set of laws banning discrimination. The struggle that lay ahead for the Negro people was a cruel one. The Leninist thesis of oppressor peoples and oppressed peoples, oppressed nations and oppressor nations, and not simply oppressed and oppressor classes in the epoch of imperialism, was fully proven in life.

As USNA imperialism tightened its murderous grip on the colonies and especially the Negro Nation, the material standard of life for the Anglo-American people began to rise. The non-exploiting classes knew instinctively that their material well-being was tied to the exploitation of the non-sovereign peoples. The exploited sections of the Anglo-American population blocked with the imperialists in the rape of the Negro Nation. If the Wall Street imperialists could not count on the support of the Anglo-American workers to brutally enforce job discrimination, housing and educational segregation and political disenfranchisement, the imperialist system could not exist.

The imperialist bribery of the Anglo-American workers made it possible and profitable to brutally murder Negro women and children, to bum their houses and churches and to meet appeals for justice with an indescribably bloody violence. There can be no doubt that history will place a collective responsibility upon the Anglo-American people for the horrors of the lynch rope and burning stake of that period.

In the face of mass starvation, "race riots," discrimination by and contempt from the vast majority of the Anglo-American people, the Negro masses plodded on. The international situation became more favorable to the struggle. Wall Street's tactic to oppose Hitler gave a moral weapon to the Negro people that they lacked before. In 1938, the courts ruled that state colleges had to admit Negroes if segregated schools were not available to them. The solid wall of reaction was beginning to crack. Under the conditions of the fascist offensive within the USNA, the militant National Negro Congress was formed in 1936. The Congress pioneered the idea of a coordinated drive by a united front of Negro organizations. They met with some notable successes. This left progressive motion forced such traitorous elements as A. Phillip Randolph and Walter White to attempt to take the hegemony of the Negro movement away from the left. The result was the 1941 March on Washington and the resulting Fair Employment Practices Commission appointed by Roosevelt. At the end of the war, the NAACP, speaking in the name of the Negro people, presented its famous *Appeal to the World, a Statement on the Denial of Human Rights to Minorities in the Case of Citizens of Negro Descent in the United States and an Appeal to the United Nations for Redress.* An embarrassed USNA government conceded that if it were to continue the ideological struggle against Communism, it would have to lend a more sympathetic ear to the demands of the Negro people. The gutter politician, Truman, was forced to appoint a Committee on Equal Rights.

Independent struggle on the part of the trade unions as well as favorable rulings by the courts, broadened the employment opportunities for Negro workers. The 1954 school decision, the anti-lynch law and in 1965 the Voting Rights Act, just about completed the victories in the legal and trade union field.

Negro Generals and Admirals no longer caused a stir by their presence. Negro politicians were to be found in the Senate and the House. Negro Mayors were elected in the large cities of the North and in a number of small southern towns. Two Negro Lt. Governors were elected in states with less than 5% Negro vote. Bull Connor is dead and Governor George Wallace has appointed a Negro to his Executive Committee.

To any fair-minded outsider, it would appear as if the battle was won. No wonder the Negro People's National Liberation Movement is in such disarray. Legally everything has been won. In fact, nothing has been won. The economic gulf between Negroes and and Anglo-Americans is wider than ever.

When the fight for fair housing began, every city had scattered pockets of poverty-stricken Negroes locked into areas of poor sanitation, no hospitals and poor schools. The so-called fair housing laws have failed to prevent the transformation of huge sections of big cities into stinking putrid slums where police murders have far outstripped the best the Klan could do. The so-called integration of the armed forces has not removed the Negro soldier from the domain of the labor battalions, but has converted him into a mercenary infantryman. The struggle to gain the equality of having Negro pilots has only added a black hand alongside of the white hand in the criminal bombing of innocent peoples.

Is it not clear to all that these goals of the struggles of the Negro masses have had the tendency to turn into their opposites? Is it not clear that the underlying cause is the colonial position of the Negro Nation? Bitter history of the struggles of all oppressed peoples surely proves that oppressed and oppressor peoples cannot be integrated. Of course there have been some gains, especially for the Negro national bourgeoisie which the government has made an effort to buy off and to a great extent has succeeded. If the Negro people were to relinquish, for one moment, the struggle to improve their lot, they would immediately be reduced to the level of slaves.

What is needed is a new perspective for the Negro People's National Liberation Movement. What is needed is the leadership of a different class.

Under the ideological leadership of the Negro "talented tenth," which could not help but be its national bourgeoisie, the goal of each class among the Negro people of achieving equality with the corresponding class of Anglo-Americans was perfectly normal since that would make the sky the limit for the Negro bourgeoisie. But inherent in this concept is that the Negro unemployed would be equal to the Anglo-American unemployed. The Negro laborer would be equal to the Anglo-American laborer. To limit the drive for liberation to such equality of poverty cannot be acceptable to the Negro masses. However, even this "equality" is impossible under capitalism.

One of the most progressive results of the past years of struggle is the massive growth in numbers of Negro industrial workers. No Anglo-American today can speak of the need of unity of the prole-

165

tariat without addressing himself first of all to the tasks of defending the Negro worker. This creates a favorable objective situation. The next step on the agenda of the Negro National Liberation Movement is to endorse and raise the goal of socialism as the only political context for the emancipation of the Negro people. Such a direction is bound to have an immediate effect upon a huge section of the working class. It is clear that the ever closer intertwining of the Negro People's movement and the vanguard of the proletariat is not only a historical inevitability, but a political necessity for either of the sections to move forward.

It is time for all militants and left progressives to carefully search out ways to raise this question within the Negro People's National Liberation Movement. Negro History Week, 1975, marks the ending of the spontaneous process of the movement. Further advances depend on consciousness, and only the revolutionaries, clearly raising, explaining and defending the goal of socialism, can create that consciousness.

ARE THERE 'RACES'?

(from the *People's Tribune*, Vol. 2, No. 7, April 1, 1975)

Are there races among human beings? Is there any connection between "race" and the national question?

All oppressing classes and nations have proclaimed their "inherent superiority" to the classes and nations they oppress. The CLP, as a part of the international proletarian revolutionary movement, the revolution that will end all oppression, stands with the great teachers of the proletariat and with all real scientists, in declaring all "racial" theories as complete nonsense and vicious lies.

Aristotle proclaimed the "superiority" of slave owners over slaves by stating that whoever "can foresee by the exercise of mind is by nature intended to be lord and master, and that which can with its body give effect to such foresight, is a subject, and by nature a slave; hence master and slave have the same interest." This old idea of the natural "inferiority" of oppressed peoples and classes did not take on a specifically "racial" tone until developing capitalist Europe launched its four century orgy of conquest, murder and enslavement of Asia, Africa and the Americas. The "scientific" theory of "races" reached its height in Nazi Germany, South Africa and the USNA. "Racial" theories are nothing but justification and covers for national oppression.

A series of studies produced by UNESCO conferences from 1949-1967, which gathered together anthropologists, biologists, sociologists and other scientists from around the world made these conclusions (reported in *Racial Discrimination,* by Hernan Santa Cruz, published by the U.N. in 1971).

1. (1949) For all practical social purposes "race" is not so much a biological phenomenon as a social myth.

2. (1964) All men living together belong to a single species and are derived from a common stock; pure races in the sense of genetically homogenous populations do not exist in the human species and there is no national, religious, geographic, linguistic, or cultural group which constitutes a race.

3. (1967) "Race," in the biological sense, is totally irrelevant to racial attitudes and thinking.

4. (1967) The division of the human species into "races" is purely arbitrary and conventional and should not imply any hierar-

chy whatsoever.

The real nature of the "scientific theories" of race can be seen in such profound statements as that of Houston Stewart Chamberlain, one of the founders of this "science," who said in discussing the difficulties of determining who was an "Aryan," "One has to use intuition or spiritual divination, this I call 'rational anthropology'." No doubt it was this rational anthropology which the Nazis used to declare the Japanese "honorary Aryans" during W.W. II. English racial "experts" declared the Welsh, Scots and Irish all to be "inferior races." The USNA Census defines "race" as follows: "The population is divided into three groups on the basis of race—white, Negro and other. Persons of Mexican birth are classified as white unless they are definitely of some other racial stock. In 1970, the father's race was used for persons of mixed parentage who were in doubt as to their classification. In 1960, persons who reported mixed parentage of white and any other race were classified according to the other race." (*U.S. Census Abstract,* 1971, p. 2)

Race theories, whether they put forward three, five or twenty-five "races" are mere matters of convenience for imperialism. They have no scientific basis—the range of physical variation within any of the so-called "races"—Caucasian, Negro, Mongoloid, Australoid, etc., is greater than the difference between the "races."

Physical differences developed as responses to various factors— skin color to the intensity of sunlight, fat distribution to the degree of cold, etc., as a product of thousands of years of isolation of peoples. Today, that isolation has ended, and with the advance of socialism which ends all national oppression, there will soon be an end to all racial theories and we shall see the blending of all these physical differences.

The only connection between "race" and national oppression is as an ideological justification for imperialism. The historical circumstance that with the exception of Japan, the major imperialist powers are "white" and the oppressed nations and peoples "colored" was trumped up into a "scientific theory" to justify the "white man's burden." The foundation of the USNA on the basis of the theft of land from the Indians and the theft of labor from the Negro slaves gave rise to the vicious white chauvinism that is the mainstay of the USNA imperialists and their justification for looting the world.

WHAT ARE NATIONAL MINORITIES?

(from the *People's Tribune,* Vol. 2, No. 10, May 15, 1975)

During the era of imperialism, one of the divisions of the world is into oppressed and oppressor nations. The oppressed nations are the source of super-profits to their imperialist oppressors who enforce their economic stranglehold and political domination of the weaker nations with military force. Under direct colonization, the imperialist power maintains total control over the exploited nation. There is no independent state. Thus, Lenin characterizes "national" uprisings within colonies as "an uprising aimed at the achievement of political independence of the oppressed nation, i.e., the establishment of a separate national state." (*A Caricature of Marxism.,* CW, Vol. 23, p. 55.)

The USNA is a multinational state, comprised of the imperialist oppressor nation, the Anglo-American nation (which consists roughly of the northern east, mid-west and western regions); its direct colonies, the Negro Nation and Puerto Rico; the oppressed Southwest region; and the Philippines, in fact a direct colony with a separate sham "state" tied openly and directly to the USNA imperialists.

As a result of imperialist oppression and exploitation, the standard of life in the colonies is driven ever downward, forcing the colonial peoples to flee impoverishment and starvation by immigrating to the oppressor nation in search of a better life. This emigration from a direct colony such as Puerto Rico and the Negro Nation is unhampered by legal hindrances; no papers are necessary, as the colonial peoples are a part of the same state. In fact, the imperialists often encourage these migrations in order to flood the labor market with "cheap labor" and thus drive down the wages of the Anglo-American proletariat.

A national minority is a person who has emigrated from a direct colony to its own imperialist oppressor nation. Irish workers are a national minority in England, but are a national group in the USNA, where the national minorities are only those people who come from the direct colonies of USNA imperialism. Thus, within the Anglo-American proletariat there are four main groupings of national minorities—those from the Negro Nation, Puerto Rico, the Philippines and the Mexican national minority from the Southwest region.

Why do we refer to some Mexican workers as a national minority, when Mexico is not a direct colony of the USNA? We do so only in regard to the Southwest region, which formerly was a part of Mexico, is a conquered territory, and was annexed by the USNA imperialists at gunpoint. Mexican workers in and from the Southwest region are a national minority within the Anglo-American proletariat. However, Mexican nationals, workers from the state of Mexico itself, are not a national minority in the Anglo-American proletariat; thus, when we refer to workers from Mexico we refer to them as "Mexican national workers."

Within the oppressor nation, the national minorities are subject to special oppression because of the colonial status of their homeland. This special oppression reinforces the oppression of the colonies and acts as a stopper to prevent too many of the colonial workers from emigrating.

In 1870, Marx wrote of this phenomenon in relation to Ireland and England:

> Every industrial and commercial centre in England now possesses a working class divided into two hostile camps, English proletarians and Irish proletarians. The ordinary English worker hates the Irish worker as a competitor who lowers his standard of life. In relation to the Irish worker he feels himself a member of the ruling nation and so turns himself into a tool of the aristocrats and capitalists of his country against Ireland, thus strengthening their domination over himself. He cherishes religious, social and national prejudices against the Irish workers... This antagonism is artificially kept alive and intensified by the press, the pulpit, the comic papers, in short by all the means at the disposal of the ruling classes. This antagonism is the secret of the impotence of the English working class, despite its organization. It is the secret by which the capitalist class maintains its power. (*Letter of Karl Marx to Meyer and Vogt,* April 8, 1870.)

The same may be said today. The strength of the imperialists lies in the historic division of the Anglo-American proletariat along national lines. This is the result of imperialist bribery, and is justified by white chauvinism. As class conscious workers, we must combat all forms of "great nation" chauvinism, the bourgeois ideology of national superiority. We must especially struggle against white chauvinism, or national superiority on the basis of skin color. It is in order to create the conditions for the unity of our class that we demand independence for the Negro Nation, Puerto Rico, and freedom for all nations oppressed by USNA imperialism; an end to deportations and the documentation of any workers; regional autonomy for the Southwest and for the Indian peoples; and equality for all national minorities! It is on this basis that we support busing and demand equal quality education for all children!

SUPPLEMENTARY CHARTS

Statistics on the Economic and Social Status of
Negroes in the USNA

Sources:

1: Black Americans, A Decade of Occupational Change, Bureau of
Labor Statistics, U.S. Department of Labor, 1972

2: The Social and Economic Status of the Black Population in the
United States, 1973, Current Population Reports, Special Studies
Series P-23, No. 48 Bureau of the Census,
U.S. Department of Commerce

3-7: Social Indicators, 1973: Statistical Policy Division, Office of
Management and Budget, U.S. Department of Commerce

Chart 9-a&b. Percent of persons employed in nonfarm occupations with earnings under \$3,000[1] in 1959 and 1969

Sex and race	1959	1969
Men	18.0	14.6
White	15.9	14.0
Negro and other races	39.5	22.1
Women	51.9	43.3
White	48.6	42.0
Negro and other races	75.3	52.0

[1] In constant 1969 dollars.

Source: U.S. Department of Commerce, Bureau of the Census, *Current Population Survey.*

Chart 10-a. Distribution of the total labor force by age, 1960, 1970, and 1980[1]

Race and age	1960	1970	1980
Negro and other	100	100	100
Under 35 years of age	42	48	55
35 years and over	58	52	45
White	100	100	100
Under 35 years of age	38	43	48
35 years and over	62	57	52

[1] Projection

Source: Travis, Sophia C. *The U.S. Labor Force Projections to 1985,* Special Labor Force Report No. 119, and U.S. Department of Labor, Bureau of Labor Statistics, *Employment and Earnings,* January 1972.

Chart 10-b. Percent with 4 years of high school or more in the civilian labor force, ages 25-34, 1970 and 1980

	Negro and other	White
1970	59	78
1980[1]	74	84

[1] Projection

Source: Johnston, Dennis, *Education of Adult Workers,* Special Labor Force Report No. 122, and William Deutermann, *Educational Attainment of Workers, March 1969 and 1970,* Special Labor Force Report No. 125.

Table 2. Distribution of the Population by Region: 1965, 1970, and 1973

Subject	1965	1970	1973
BLACK			
United States millions..	20.9	22.6	23.2
Percent, total	100	100	100
South	54	53	52
North	38	39	40
Northeast	18	19	19
North Central	20	20	21
West	8	8	8
WHITE			
United States millions	169.2	177.7	180.3
Percent, total	100	100	100
South	27	28	29
North	55	54	53
Northeast	26	25	25
North Central	29	29	29
West	17	18	18

Table 89. Black Elected Officials by State: March 1974

State	1970 percent black	Black elected officials					
		Total	Congress	State	City	County	Other
United States	11.1	2,991	17	239	1,360	242	1,133
Maine	0.3	5	–	1	3	–	1
New Hampshire	0.3	1	–	–	–	–	1
Vermont	0.2	2	–	–	1	–	1
Massachusetts	3.1	23	1	5	10	–	7
Rhode Island	2.7	7	–	1	2	–	4
Connecticut	6.0	50	–	6	31	–	13
New York	11.9	174	2	14	18	9	131
New Jersey	10.7	152	–	7	61	4	80
Pennsylvania	8.6	83	1	14	19	2	47
Ohio	9.1	139	1	11	85	3	39
Indiana	6.9	55	–	7	27	3	18
Illinois	12.8	152	2	19	73	3	55
Michigan	11.2	194	2	14	73	28	77
Wisconsin	2.9	14	–	3	6	3	2
Minnesota	0.9	8	–	2	1	–	5
Iowa	1.2	9	–	1	3	–	5
Missouri	10.3	93	1	15	47	4	26
NorthDakota	0.4	–	–	–	–	–	–
South Dakota	0.2	–	–	–	–	–	–

Nebraska	2.7	2	–	1	–	–	1
Kansas	4.8	25	–	5	11	1	8
Delaware	14.3	8	–	3	5	–	–
Maryland	17.8	65	1	19	32	1	12
District of Columbia	71.1	8	1	–	–	–	7
Virginia	18.5	63	–	2	39	17	5
West Virginia	3.9	5	–	1	4	–	–
North Carolina	22.2	159	–	3	113	7	36
South Carolina	30.5	116	–	3	57	20	36
Georgia	25.9	137	1	16	72	9	39
Florida	15.3	73	–	3	65	1	4
Kentucky	7.2	59	–	3	43	2	11
Tennessee	15.8	87	–	9	27	29	22
Alabama	26.2	149	–	3	57	17	72
Mississippi	36.8	191	–	1	91	26	73
Arkansas	18.3	150	–	4	74	20	52
Louisiana	29.8	149	–	8	42	32	67
Oklahoma	6.7	66	–	4	40	–	22
Texas	12.5	124	1	8	59	–	56
Montana	0.3	–	–	–	–	–	–
Idaho	0.3	1	–	–	1	–	–
Wyoming	0.8	1	–	–	1	–	–
Colorado	3.0	13	–	4	5	–	4
New Mexico	1.9	4	–	1	3	–	–
Arizona	3.0	10	–	2	2	–	6
Utah	0.6	–	–	–	–	–	–
Nevada	5.7	6	–	3	–	1	2
Washington	2.1	15	–	2	7	–	6
Oregon	1.3	6	–	1	1	–	4
California	7.0	132	3	8	48	–	73
Alaska	3.0	6	–	2	1	–	3
Hawaii	1.0	–	–	–	–	–	–

3.
VICTIMS OF FORCIBLE RAPE, ROBBERY, AND AGGRAVATED ASSAULT, BY RACE AND SEX: 1965
(Rate per 100,000 population)

Crime	White		Negro and other races	
	Male	Female	Male	Female
Forcible rape	(x)	50	(x)	193
Robbery	97	43	174	270
Aggravated assault	297	71	305	386

X Not applicable.

Source: Philip H. Ennis, Criminal Victimization in the United States: A Report of a National Survey, 1967 (a report of a research study submitted to the President's Commission on Law Enforcement and Administration of Justice, Field Survey No. 2).

175

VICTIMS OF HOMICIDE: 1940-1971
By Race and Sex
(Rate per 100,000 population)

Year	All races	White		Negro and other races	
		Male	Female	Male	Female
1940	6.3	5.0	1.4	55.5	13.0
1941	6.0	4.5	1.3	55.0	12.6
1942	5.9	4.4	1.3	53.5	12.1
1943	5.1	4.2	1.2	42.5	9.9
1944	5.0	4.0	1.2	44.1	9.7
1945	5.7	4.9	1.3	48.0	10.7
1946	6.4	4.9	1.5	54.4	12.4
1947	6.1	4.8	1.5	51.5	11.9
1948	5.9	4.5	1.5	51.0	11.7
1949	5.4	4.1	1.4	45.8	11.4
1950	5.3	3.9	1.4	45.5	11.2
1951	4.9	3.6	1.4	41.3	10.7
1952	5.2	3.7	1.3	45.4	10.8
1953	4.8	3.5	1.4	41.3	9.6
1954	4.8	3.5	1.4	40.6	9.5
1955	4.5	3.4	1.2	36.9	9.5
1956	4.6	3.3	1.3	37.1	10.3
1957	4.5	3.2	1.3	36.5	9.2
1958	4.5	3.4	1.4	34.9	9.3
1959	4.6	3.5	1.4	35.0	9.4
1960	4.7	3.6	1.4	34.5	9.9
1961	4.7	3.6	1.5	33.5	8.9
1962	4.8	3.8	1.6	35.5	8.9
1963	4.9	3.9	1.5	35.7	9.0
1964	5.1	3.9	1.6	37.4	9.2
1965	5.5	4.4	1.6	40.0	10.0
1966	5.9	4.5	1.8	43.4	10.6
1967	6.8	5.3	1.9	49.5	11.9
1968	7.3	5.9	1.9	54.6	11.7
19 9	7.7	6.0	2.0	58.1	11.7
1970*	7.6	6.4	2.0	56.2	10.6
1971	8.5	7.0	2.3	60.3	12.7

MEDIAN EARNINGS, BY OCCUPATION, SEX, AND RACE: 1971

(For Year-Round Full-Time Workers)
(Dollars)

Occupation[1]	Male			Female		
	Total	White	Negro	Total	White	Negro
All workers	9,399	9,659	6,669	5,593	5,641	5,014
Professional and technical workers	12,518	12,629	10,046	8,312	8,294	8,298
Farmers and farm managers	4,308	4,356	(NA)	(NA)	(NA)	(NA)
Managers and administrators, except farm	12,721	12,781	9,867	6,738	6,690	(NA)
Clerical workers	9,124	9,257	7,742	5,696	5,685	5,779
Sales workers	10,650	10,769	(NA)	4,485	4,448	(NA)
Craftsmen, foremen	9,627	9,749	7,556	5,425	5,511	(NA)
Operatives	7,915	8,198	6,188	4,789	4,825	4,448
Private household workers	(NA)	(NA)	(NA)	1,926	1,870	1,895
Service workers, except private household	7,111	7,560	5,566	4,159	4,169	4,039
Farm laborers	3,752	4,134	(NA)	(NA)	(NA)	(NA)
Nonfarm laborers	6,866	7,129	5,990	4,548	4,645	(NA)

NA Not available.

[1] Occupation of longest job.

Source: Bureau of the Census, Current Population Reports, Series P-60, No. 85.

5.

HOUSEHOLDS LIVING IN CROWDED CONDITIONS, BY INCOME AND RACE: 1970

Family income	All races Number (thousands)	Percent	White and other races Number (thousands)	Percent	Negro Number (thousands)	Percent
All households	5,060	8.0	3,862	6.7	1,199	19.4
Less than $2,000	392	.5.1	221	3.5	171	12.3
$2,000 to $2,999	253	6.6	144	4.5	110	18.4
$3,000 to $3,999	325	8.9	197	6.4	128	22.8
$4,000 to $4,999	346	9.8	226	7.5	121	24.0
$5,000 to $5,999	386	10.2	271	8.3	115	23.8
$6,000 to $6,999	396	10.2	294	8.6	102	23.0
$7,000 to $9,999	1,161	9.7	935	8.6	226	22.3
$10,000 to $14,999	1,173	8.2	1,013	7.5	160	19.8
$15,000 and over	628	5.8	561	5.4	67	17.4

Note: Income is 1969 family income,
Source: Bureau of the Census, 1970 Census of Housing, Vol. II, Part 1.

HOUSEHOLDS LIVING IN SUBSTANDARD UNITS, BY RACE: 1950-1970

Race	1950	1960	1970[1]
NUMBER (thousands)			
All races	4,794	8,474	4,740
White	2,126	6,210	3,303
Negro and other races	2,667	2,263	1,437
PERCENT			
All races	35.4	16.0	7.4
White	31.8	13.0	5.7
Negro and other races	73.2	44.0	23.0

[1] In 1970 "Negro and other races" is limited to Negro only and "white" includes white and other races.
Source: Bureau of the Census, 1950 Census of Housing. Vol. I, Part 1; 1960 Census of Housing, Vol. I, Part 1; 1970 Components of Inventory Change Survey, unpublished data.

6.

READING ACHIEVEMENT: 1971
(Group Differences From the Performance of All 17-Year-Olds)

Characteristic	Percent above or below average performance of all 17-year-olds
SEX	
Male	-2.0
Female	1.9
COLOR	
White	2.2
Black	-16.4
EDUCATION OF PARENT	
No high school	-11.1
Some high school	-6.0
High school graduate	-.3
Post-high school	5.6
SIZE AND TYPE OF COMMUNITY	
Low metro	-7.7
Main big city	1.3
Urban fringe	1.2
High metro	5.6
Medium city	.8
Small places	-1.4
Rural	-2.6

SCIENCE ACHIEVEMENT: 1970

(Group Differences From the Performance of All 17-Year-Olds)

Characteristic	Percent above or below average performance of all 17-year-olds
SEX	
Male	2.8
Female	-2.4
COLOR	
White	2.0
Black	-11.9
EDUCATION OF PARENT	
No high school	-8.4
Some high school	-7.7
High school graduate	.1
Post-high school	5.0
SIZE AND TYPE OF COMMUNITY	
Low metro	-7.4
Main big city	.2
Urban fringe	.9
High metro	5.1
Medium city	1.2
Small places	-1.5
Rural	-3.6

Age and year	Number of persons with at least 4 years of high school (thousands)			Percent of persons with at least 4 years of high school		
	All races	White	Negro and other races	All races	White	Negro and other races
PERSONS 20 YEARS OLD AND OVER						
1940	23,142	22,446	695	26.8	28.7	8.7
1950	35,205	33,807	1,398	35.6	37.8	14.8
1960	47,690	45,002	2,688	43.3	45.4	24.0
1962	54,119	51,049 5	3,070	48.5	50.9	27.0
1964	58,017	4,402	3,615	50.6	52.9	30.7
1965	59,928	56,179	3,749	51.7	54.0	31.4
1966	61,499	57,558	3,941	52.7	55.0	32.7
1967	63,951	59,677	4,274	54.0	56.2	34.9
1968	67,109	62,553	4,556	56.2	57.8	36.3
1969	69,811	64,961	4,849	57.0	59.2	38.0
1970	72,913	67,559	5,357	58.4	60.5	40.6
1971	75,934	70,212	5,722	59.7	61.8	42.2
1972	78,908	72,895	6,015	61.5	63.6	43.7
PERSONS 20 TO 24 YEARS OLD						
1940	5,108	4,923	185	44.1	47.6	14.8
1950	5,998	5,674	324	52.4	56.0	24.9
1960	6,867	6,313	554	63.6	66.6	41.9
1962	7,470	6,880	590	68.1	71.7	42.9
1964	8,859	8,070	789	72.3	75.0	52.7
1965	9,344	8,566	778	73.2	76.3	50.2
1966	9,661	8,804	857	75.0	77.9	54.2
1967	10,314	9,385	929	76.0	78.8	56.4
1968	11,080	10,020	1,060	77.5	80.0	59.9
1969	11,577	10,498	1,079	78.3	81.1	58.6
1970	12,554	11,234	1,320	80.5	82.7	65.8
1971	13,511	12,055	1,456	81.4	83.5	67.6
1972	14,256	12,775	1,484	82.7	84.9	67.9

FOOTNOTES

Definitions

(1) Lenin, Vladimir I., *Imperialism, the Highest Stage of Capitalism*, Foreign Languages Press, Peking, 1965, p. 106.

(2) Marx, Karl, *Capital, Vol. I,* Progress Publishers, Moscow, 1971, pp. 667, 668, 669.

(3) Lenin, Vladimir I., *Lenin on the Struggle Against Revisionism,* Proletarian Publishers, 1975, pp. 3-4.

(4) *Imperialism, the Highest Stage of Capitalism, Op. Cit.,* pp. 97, 101.

Chapter 1

(1) Marx, Karl, *Theories of Surplus Value, Part II,* Progress Publishers, Moscow, 1968, pp. 302-303.

(2) Marx, Karl, *Capital, Vol. III,* Progress Publishers, Moscow, 1971, p. 804.

(3) *Ibid.,* p. 326.

(4) Aptheker, Herbert, *A Documentary History of the Negro People in the United States,* Citadel Press, New York, 1967, pp. 247, 248.

(5) Marx, Karl, *Capital, Vol. I,* Progress Publishers, Moscow, 1971, pp. 253-54.

(6) *Ibid.,* p. 226.

(7) *Ibid.,* p. 226.

(8) Marx, Karl, *The Poverty of Philosophy* (in *Handbook of Marxism*), Martin Lawrence Ltd., London, 1935, pp. 356-357.

(9) *Capital, Vol. I, Op. Cit.,* p. 711.

(10) *Ibid.* p. 191.

(11) Stampp, Kenneth M., *The Peculiar Institution,* Vintage Books, New York, 1956, pp. 62, 65.

Chapter 2

(1) Marx, Karl and Engels, Frederick, *The Civil War in the United States,* International Publishers, New York, 1969, p. 73.

(2) Stampp, Kenneth, *The Peculiar Institution,* Vintage Books, New York, 1956, pp. 30, 38.

(3) Marx, Karl, *The Poverty of Philosophy* (in *Handbook of*

Marxism), Martin Lawrence Ltd., London, 1935, pp. 356-357.
(4) *The Civil War in the United States, Op. Cit.,* pp. 63-64.
(5) *Ibid.,* pp. 67-68.

Chapter 3

(1) Stalin, Joseph, *Marxism and the National Colonial Question,* Proletarian Publishers, San Francisco, 1975, p. 117.
(2) *Ibid.,* p. 112.
(3) Woodson and Wesley, *The Negro in Our History,* Associated Publishers, New York, 1966, p. 415.
(4) Marx, Karl and Engels, Fredrick, *The Civil War in the United States,* International Publishers, New York, 1969, p. 245.
(5) Woodson, Comer Van, *Origins of the New South, 1877- 1913,* Louisiana State University Press, Baton Rouge, 1951, pp. 179, 196.
(6) Foster, William Z., *The Negro People in American History,* International Publishers, New York, 1954, pp. 327, 333.
(7) Kuczynski and Witt, *The Economics of Barbarism,* International Publishers, New York, 1940, pp. 50, 52.
(8) Dimitroff, Georgi, *The United Front Against Fascism,* Proletarian Publishers, San Francisco, 1975, pp. 10, 12, 14-15.
(9) *The Negro People in American History, Op. Cit.,* pp. 381, 384.
(10) *The Negro in Our History, Op, Cit.,* p. 554.
(11) War of Rebellion, Congressional Inquiry, Vol. 33.
(12) *The Negro People in American History, Op. Cit.,* p. 534.
(13) *Ibid.,* p. 441.
(14) Haywood, Harry, *Negro Liberation,* International Publishers, New York, 1948, p. 172.
(15) *The Negro People in American History, Op. Cit.,* p. 413.
(16) *Ibid.,* pp. 417, 418.
(17) *Ibid.,* pp. 356, 355.
(18) *The Negro in Our History, Op. Cit.,* p. 538.
(19) *The Negro People in American History, Op. Cit.,* pp. 423, 422.
(18) The Negro in Our History, Op. Cit., p. 538.
(19) *The Negro People in American History, Op. Cit.,* pp. 423, 422.
(20) *The Negro in Our History, Op. Cit.,* p. 545.
(21) Editors, *Political Affairs,* October, 1965, p. 7.
(22) Taylor, William C., *Political Affairs,* October, 1965, p. 7.

Chapter 4

(1) Stalin, Joseph, *Marxism and the National-Colonial Question,* Proletarian Publishers, San Francisco, 1975, p. 28.

(2) *Ibid.,* p. 31.

(3) Lenin, Vladimir I., *Selections from V. I. Lenin and J. V. Stalin on the National Colonial Question,* Calcutta Book House, Calcutta, 1970, p. 14.

(4) *Marxism and the National Colonial Question, Op. Cit.,* p. 22.

(5) Lenin, Vladimir I., *Critical Remarks on the National Question,* Foreign Language Publishing House, Moscow, 1954, p. 59.

(6) *Newsweek,* October 19, 1970, p. 50.

(7) *Marxism and the National Colonial Question, Op. Cit.,* p. 60.

(8) *Ibid.,* p. 297.

(9) *Ibid.,* p. 21.

(10) Du Bois, W. E. B., *Souls of Black Folk,* Fawcett Publications, Inc., New York, 1968, p. 182.

(11) *Ibid.,* p. 141.

Chapter 5

(1) Stalin, Joseph, *Marxism and the National Colonial Question,* Proletarian Publishers, San Francisco, 1975, pp. 175-177.

(2) *Ibid.,* pp. 288-290.

Chapter 6

(1) Marx, Karl, *Capital, Vol. I,* Progress Publishers, Moscow, 1971, p. 705.

(2) Foster, William Z., *Political Affairs,* July, 1953, p. 17.

(3) Lenin, V. I., *Questions of National Policy and Proletarian Internationalism,* Progress Publishers, Moscow, 1970, p. 92.

(4) *Ibid.,* p. 108.

(5) *Ibid.,* p. 64-65.

(6) *Ibid.,* p. 72.

(7) *Ibid.,* p. 72.

(8) *Ibid.,* pp. 73-74.

(9) *Capital, Vol. I, Op. Cit.,* p. 284.

(10) *Questions of National Policy and Proletarian Internationalism, Op. Cit.,* p. 107.

(11) Marx, Karl and Engels, Frederick, *Selected Correspondence,* Progress Publishers, Moscow, 1965, pp. 231-232.

(12) *Questions of National Policy and Proletarian Internationalism, Op. Cit.,* p. 26.

(13) *Ibid.,* p. 27.

(14) Stalin, Joseph, *Marxism and the National Colonial Question,* Proletarian Publishers, San Francisco, 1975, pp. 57-58.

(15) *Ibid.,* pp. 72-73.

(16) Lenin, V. I., *Collected Works,* Vol. XIX, International Publishers, New York, 1942, pp. 292-293.

Chapter 7

(1) Foster, William Z., *The Negro People in American History,* International Publishers, New York, 1970, p. 359.

(2) Report of the National Emergency Committee to the President on Economic Conditions in the South.

(3) Boyer, R.D., and Morais, H.M., *Labor's Untold Story,* United Electrical Workers, New York, 1970.

(4) *Reported Voter Registration for Persons of Voting Age, By Region: 1972,* U.S. Department of Commerce, Social and Economic Statistics Administration, Bureau of the Census.

(5) *1970 Statistical Abstract,* Table No. 556, p. 369, "Voter Registration."

(6) *Characteristics of the Population, "Industry and Income Based on Race,"* U.S. Dept, of Commerce, Social and Economic Statistics Administration, Bureau of the Census, 1970.

(7) *Median Income of Families: 1972,* U.S. Department of Commerce, Social and Economic Statistics Administration, Bureau of the Census.

(8) *Directory of National and International Labor Unions in the U.S.,* U.S. Department of Labor, Bureau of Labor Statistics, p. 58.

(9) Mann, Charles P., *Stalin's Though Illuminates Problems of Negro Freedom Struggles,* Educational Department of the CPUSA, 1954, p. 21.

Chapter 8

(1) Spero, S. O., and Harris, Al, *The Black Worker,* Columbia University Press, 1931, p. 220.

(2) *Ibid.,* pp., 77, 314.

(3) *Ibid.,* p. 257.

(4) *See* Foster, William Z., *The Negro People in American History,* International Publishers, New York, 1970, p. 499.

(5) Marx, Karl and Engels, Frederick, *Manifesto of the Communist Party,* Foreign Languages Press, Peking, 1968, p. 39.

(6) Morgan, J. A., et. al., *Income and Welfare in the U.S.,* Anchor Books, New York, 1963, p. 56.

(7) *Report of the President's Committee on Equal Employment Opportunity,* U.S. Government Printing Office, 1963, p. 50.

(8) Jacobsen, U., *The Negro and the American Labor Movement,* Anchor Books, New York, 1968, p. 256.

Chapter 9

(1) Lenin, V. I., *Questions of National Policy and Proletarian Internationalism,* Progress Publishers, Moscow, 1970, pp. 42-43.

(2) Foster, William Z., *The Negro People in American History,* International Publishers, New York, 1970, pp. 381-383.

(3) Haywood, Harry, *Negro Liberation,* International Publishers, New York, 1948, pp. 207-208

Chapter 10

(1) Engels, Frederick, *Anti-Dühring,* International Publishers, New York, 1939, p. 117.

INDEX

A

Algeria, 59
American Exceptionalism, 5, 9, 45, 93
Anderson, John R., 20
Anglo-America, 3
Anglo-American Nation, 3, 4, 9, 37, 62, 75, 82, 83, 84, 98, 105, 106, 117, 119, 121, 123, 124, 125, 127, 129, 130
Anglo-American proletariat, 1, 75, 97, 132, 169, 170
Anglo-European, 4, 9, 11, 60, 62, 89, 91, 126
Aptheker, Herbert, 31, 53, 183

B

"Battle for Democracy", 31, 45
Beatles, The, 83
Black Belt, 11, 12, 13, 14, 15, 16, 18, 19, 29, 38, 39, 59, 62, 67, 68, 70, 79, 81, 103, 107, 117, 126, 135, 137, 139, 140, 141, 142, 143, 144, 145, 146, 147, 148, 150, 151, 162
Blase, Cole, 37
Boll Weevil, 79
Bond, Julian, 71
Breckinridge, 26
Browder, Earl, 5, 45
Brown, John, 23, 24, 26, 29
Brotherhood of Timberworkers, 129
Buchanan, 26
Butler, General, 29

C

Capitalist slavery, 14-21
Carnegie Steel Co., 119
Chambers Brothers, 83
CIA, 55
CIO, 50, 119, 129, 131
Colored National Labor Union, 33
Communist International, 1, 59, 133, 151
Communist Labor Party, 1, 28, 59, 97, 125, 131, 132, 133
Congress (of USNA), 10, 29, 71, 106
Coolidge, Calvin, 41
cotton, 14, 15, 16, 17, 18, 19, 21, 23, 24, 34, 60, 68, 69, 70, 75, 77, 79, 80, 104
CPUSA, 5, 7, 9, 32, 35, 39, 44, 45, 46, 50, 52, 59, 79, 93, 132, 133, 160, 162, 186

D

Davis, Ben, 44, 160
Dennis, Eugene, 31, 160
Detroit uprising, 53
Douglas, Stephen, 26
Douglass, Frederick, 30
Du Pont family, 48, 104
DuBois, W. E. B., 27, 43, 44, 46, 47, 48, 49, 82, 97

E

Eastland, James, 97, 98, 107
Eisenhower, Dwight, 55
Engels, Frederick, 22, 32, 59,

87, 131, 183, 184, 186, 187
Equal Rights Commission, 120
Equal Rights League, 48
Evers, Charles, 71

F

Farmers Alliance, 33, 36, 38
Fascism, 34, 37, 38, 184
Fifteenth Amendment, 10
Fifth Dimension, 83
Firestone, Harvey, 48
Foster, Steven, 83
Foster, William Z., 5, 9, 31,
   32, 38, 43, 44, 45, 46, 48,
   93, 160
Fourteenth Amendment, 10
Fulbright, William, 107

G

Goode, Eslanda, 44
Grant, U.S., 34, 35

H

Harding, Warren G., 41
Harris, Joel Chandler, 84
Hayes-Tilden Agreement, 32,
   35, 36
Haywood, Harry, 43, 44
Hendrix, Jimi, 83
Henry, John, 84
Hindenburg, Paul, 36
Hitler, Adolph, 29, 36, 37, 38,
   39, 164
Hughes, Langston, 16, 17, 19,
   20, 44, 45, 49, 61, 128, 161
Imperialism, 5, 6, 8, 58, 90,
   129, 183

I

Indian Peoples, 3, 4, 6, 11, 46,
   58, 60, 71, 90, 91, 126, 136,
   168, 171
Indigo, 67
International Workingman's
   Association (First
   International), 33
Ireland, 62, 92, 94, 99, 162,
   170

J

Jackson, James, 44, 160, 162
Johnson, Andrew, 29, 30
Johnson, L. B., 52, 56
Johnson, Leroy, 71
Jolson, Al, 83
Jones, Tom, 83
Juarez, Benito, 92

K

Kansas, 26
Kansas-Nebraska Act, 24
Kennedy, J.F., 55, 56
King, M. L. Jr., 47, 75
Ku Klux Klan (KKK), 29, 32,
   33, 36, 38, 127, 129, 148

L

Lenin, V. I., 1, 5, 7, 8, 38, 59,
   68, 77, 94, 95, 100, 102,
   126, 146, 148, 155, 160,
   169, 183, 185, 186, 187
Liberal founders of NAACP,
   48
Lincoln, Abraham, 24, 26, 29,
   92

Lovestone, Jay, 5, 45, 140
Lumumba, Patrice, 44

M

Maddox, Lester, 71
Mann, Charles P., 44, 115
Mao Tsetung, 59, 77, 94
Marx, Karl, 7, 13, 15, 16, 17,
    18, 22, 23, 26, 32, 33, 59,
    94, 97, 99, 119, 170, 183,
    184, 185, 186, 187
Massell, Sam, 71
McCormick, Mrs. Cyrus, 48
McCown, John L., 71
Mellon, 104
Missouri Compromise, 24, 26
Mobuto, Joseph, 44, 70
Morgan, J. P., 69, 103, 104,
    118
multinational state, 60, 169
Mussolini, Benito, 38, 39

N

NAACP, 48, 120, 164
national chauvinism, 9, 89
national cultural autonomy,
    100, 101
National Independent Political
    Rights League, 46
National Negro Congress, 119,
    164
nations, 58
Negro, 10
Negro bourgeoisie, 40, 42, 43,
    44, 46, 47, 48, 50, 71, 73,
    162, 165
Negro church, 41, 42, 82
Negro farmers, 46, 77, 80, 141,
    142
Negro Labor Councils, 52

Negro Nation, 3, 9, 11, 12, 13,
    19, 21, 27, 37, 38, 43, 45,
    53, 59, 62, 63, 68, 70, 71,
    73, 74, 75, 79, 81, 82, 83,
    84, 92, 95, 96, 97, 99, 100,
    102, 103, 104, 105, 106,
    107, 108, 109, 110, 115,
    116, 117, 118, 119, 122,
    124, 125, 126, 127, 129,
    130, 131, 132, 133, 162,
    163, 165, 166, 169, 171
Negro People's Convention
    Movement, 31
Negro proletariat, 50, 52, 57,
    74, 75, 80, 140, 148, 156
neo-colonialism, 47, 55, 56
New York Communist Clubs,
    132
Niagara Movement, 48
Northrup, Soloman, 14

O

October Revolution, 28

P

Pan-African Movement, 47,
    153
Panama Canal Zone, 3
patriarchal slavery, 13, 18, 29
Perry, Pettis, 44, 160
Philippine Islands, 3, 169
Phillips, Wendel, 30
Populism, 34, 36-40
Presley, Elvis, 83
primitive accumulation, 6, 7
Puerto Rico, 3, 59, 81, 162,
    169, 171

R

race, 10, 30, 41, 43, 46, 59, 60,
    93, 94, 118, 131, 135, 136,
    152, 154, 157, 164, 167,
    168
Republican Party, 24, 26, 33,
    35
rice, 15, 75
Robeson, Paul, 44
Rockefeller family, 103, 104,
    118
Roosevelt, Teddy, 92

S

Scott, Dred, 9, 26
semi-colony, 8
Sheridan, General, 29
Sherman, General, 42
Sly and the Family Stone, 83
South (definition), 103
Southern Farmers Alliance, 33
Stalin, J.V., 1, 28, 59, 60, 75,
    81, 84, 85, 86, 94, 101, 115,
    116, 159, 160, 184, 185,
    186
Stennis, John, 107
Stevens, Thaddeus, 30
Strikes in Negro Nation, 74
sugar, 17, 68, 75
Sumner, Charles, 30

T

Taney, Roger B., 10
Taylor, William C., 52, 53
Thirteenth Amendment, 10, 31
Tillman, Ben, 36, 37, 38, 39

tobacco, 21, 67, 69, 75, 77, 80
Toombs, Senator, 26
Tredegar Iron Co., 20

U

Unemployed Councils, 119,
    129
Union Leagues, 33, 38
United Mine Workers, 117,
    129
United Nations, 100, 164
Urban League, 120
USNA imperialism, 4, 6, 11,
    41, 55, 59, 69, 70, 75, 92,
    93, 103, 107, 125, 130, 131,
    132, 163, 169, 171
USNA state, 3, 93, 103, 108-9,
    117, 122, 125, 131

V

Vardman, 37
Vietnam, 55

W

Washington, Booker T., 44, 47
Washington, Walter, 71
Watson, Tom, 36, 38
Watts, 52, 53, 162
white chauvinism, 9, 89-100,
    119, 124, 125, 134, 150,
    154, 155, 168, 170
white supremacy, 7-8, 9, 14,
    33, 34, 37, 89-94
Wilson, Charles, 105
World Court, 100

Made in the USA
Columbia, SC
26 February 2019